THE WORKS

OF THE

ENEMY

(SATAN AND HIS DEMONIC FORCES)

The Work of Satan

Robert Antwi

authorHOUSE®

AuthorHouse™
1663 Liberty Drive
Bloomington, IN 47403
www.authorhouse.com
Phone: 1 (800) 839-8640

Published by AuthorHouse 02/24/2015

ISBN: 978-1-4969-7263-7 (sc)
ISBN: 978-1-4969-7264-4 (e)

Contents

THE WORKS OF THE ENEMY (SATAN AND HIS FORCES)

"He that committeth sin is of the devil; for the devil sinneth from the beginning. For this purpose the Son of God was manifested, that he might destroy the works of the devil." (1 Jon 3:8)

Dedication

I dedicate this book to my children, Isaac, Abigail, and Jedidah, who have been my prayer partners in good and rough times. I love my kids for they are on fire for the Lord Jesus. They pray and read their Bible almost every day and are excited for Sundays, because they can go to church. I pray for my kids and they have grown up to be godly children. Looking, at Lamentations 2: 19 "Arise, cry out in the night: in the beginning of the watches pour out thine heart like water before the face of the Lord: lift up thy hands toward him for the life of thy young children, that faint for hunger in the top of every street", God is calling on every Christian parent to rise up during the early morning hours to pray for your kids. I put it to test and it has work for me. Our children are faint for the word of God, righteousness, and respect for the elderly. We need to teach our children the word of God and pray for them to live a life worthy of the vocation of their calling. Isaac, Abigail and Jedidah are good kids and it is my prayer that goodness and mercy shall follow them all the days of their life and they will dwell in the house of the Lord, forever and ever.

Introduction

Satan and his forces are waging a war against humanity but the sad thing is many Christians are not aware of the extent of this warfare. The Bible teaches a lot about the works of the enemy, so I decided to write on this topic to bring light to what Satan and his forces are doing in this world, countries, communities, societies, cities, towns and in individual's life. I went to a Seminary Library to look for books on this topic but all the books on Satan and his demonic forces were very old. I will do my best to write as much as I can on the works of the enemy, backing every work of the enemy, with the Word of God. Satan and his forces are working twenty four hours a day, seven days a week, four weeks a month and twelve months a year. They work all the year, without any vacation. The major work of the enemy is to get Christians to sin against God and to diminish their faith in God. In the world Satan is using, money, sex and power to keep many people from knowing God, through His Son Jesus Christ. Money is the root of all evil, so many evil and untold hardship come to fruitful in the name of money. Satan and his forces are working in all the four corners around the world to keep people away from knowing God. One may be praying on a topic for a long time without any answer, then, the enemy will tell you that your God cannot answer your prayers, and if you listen to the enemy, then your faith in God will diminish. Whatever, God hates is what Satan loves, for example, God says, "I hate divorce" and Satan will say, "I love divorce." Satan may keep you not only in poverty, but in debt. Satan may take away your health, which may come along with sadness and depression. Satan is crafty and cunning so we may only attack him in the name, which is above any other name in heaven, or on earth or under the earth, which is Jesus Christ. As you read on, you are going to see how the enemy is fighting the spiritual warfare with his demonic forces. The Bible tells us how Christians will be able to wage this spiritual warfare against Satan and his forces. Looking at Ephesians 6:12-17 "For we wrestle not against flesh and blood, but against principalities, against powers, against the rulers of the darkness of this world, against spiritual wickedness in high places. Wherefore take unto you the whole armour of God, that ye may be able to withstand in the evil day, and having done all, to stand. Stand therefore, having your loins girt about with truth, and having on the breastplate of righteousness; And your feet shod with the preparation of the gospel of peace; And above all, taking the shield of faith, wherewith ye shall be able to quench all the fiery darts of the wicked. And take the helmet of salvation, and the sword of the Spirit, which is the word of God." Christians are to put on the armour, of truth, righteousness, the gospel of peace, faith, helmet of salvation and the word of God, in order to wage the spiritual warfare against Satan and his forces. This will be more explained as you read on. It is my prayer that you will be able to know more about the works of the enemy and be able to pray effectively to destroy the works of the enemy in your life and the world around you.

Chapter One

The Works of the Enemy

Who is the enemy? Christians have to know the enemy they are dealing with and his power in order to stand firm in Jesus Christ to destroy the works of the enemy. The enemy is not your mother, father, sister, brother, wife, husband, boss at work or friend, although the enemy could use anyone who will allow himself or herself to fight against you. The enemy is Satan and his team of fallen angels, which Satan has divided into four battalions to fight humankind (Christians and non-Christians). "The Bible nowhere enters into an argument to prove the person and being of God. It assumes His being and reveals His person and character. Without preface or introduction, the Bible brings God before us in all His majesty and omnipotence. God is at the world's beginning, and He it was who created the beginning of all things. "In the beginning God created the heaven and earth." How sublime and awe-inspiring our first glimpse of God! God is revealed not by argument but by work. We learn what He is from what he does. In like manner is the revelation of the devil. He is before us in full person without introduction or ceremony as the evil one, a graduate in the works of guile and evil. The curtain is drawn and the chief actor is in full dress. A world is at stake, man is to be seduced, Eden is blasted. No light is shed upon his past history, no knowledge of the school where he learned his dire trade. He was before earthly life. Eden does not date his birth, and is not the first chapter of his history, nor is it the first trial of his hellish art. We have no access to the archives of the past. Eden bounds our horizon, and the devil is there. Henceforth his history is to run parallel with our race. Man is to be the object of his schemes, his ruin, and his ambition. Earth is to be the favorite scene of his exploits. He is at the cradle of man, and has much to do in shaping his character and determining his destiny.[1] Little is known of his beginning and Isaiah talk about his fall from heaven. Isaiah 14:12-15 "How art thou fallen from heaven, O Lucifer, son of the morning! How art thou cut down to the ground, which didst weaken the nations! For thou hast said in thine heart, I will ascend into heaven, I will exalt my throne above the stars of God: I will sit also upon the mount of the congregation, in the sides of the north: I will ascend above the heights of the clouds: I will be like the most High. Yet thou shalt be brought down to hell, to the sides of the pit." The dazzling quality of angelic perfection would seem to preclude the very thought of sin. Yet the ennobling fact is that heaven is not only given; it is also earned. Lucifer was created in sanctifying grace to crown his natural perfection; he was, that is, fully equipped to win the prize of heaven, but he still has to win it. Because he could win, he could also lose. Like our own, his freedom was reverently respected by the action of God; and like ourselves, if he were to have heaven he would have to merit it by the goodness of a free act, by his own free choice. Because the gate of heaven were thrown open to his efforts it became possible for him to go to hell. In this supreme test, the devil did not win heaven but lost it; or rather, he freely and deliberately turned his back on it. He was the first; all others who joined his hordes, whether from among the angels or from among men, were volunteers, haunting the halls of hell only because they so chose.[2] Lucifer which was the name of the angel of beauty, wisdom and power, but fell from heaven as he decided to usurp the throne of the Most High God and to demand to be worshiped like God. Lucifer decided to exalt his throne above the stars of God for he wanted to be like the Most High God. He wanted to be worshiped. This unlawful act of Lucifer brought a war in heaven. Looking at Rev. 12:7-9 "And there was war in heaven: Michael and his angels fought against the dragon; and the dragon fought and his angels. And prevailed not; neither was their place found any more in heaven. And the great dragon was cast out, that old Serpent, called the Devil, and Satan, which deceiveth the whole world; he was cast out into the earth, and his angels were cast out with him." Lucifer who latter on turned out to be the great dragon, the Devil, Old Serpent and Satan, because of jealousy and pride, is doing his best to get as many people who will join him and he will send them into doom which is for him and his fallen angels. Satan was able to deceived 1/3 of the angels to follow him. Do not take this lightly for Satan is able to deceive any person, even a Christian who is not walking worthy of the vocation of his/her calling. Lucifer was turned into the great dragon and he lost his beauty but not his wisdom and power. Satan is so wise and powerful that every child of God has to be very careful when dealing with this dragon. Satan has divided the fallen angels into four battalions to fight his war against the human race. Satan knew that if he was able to deceive the first human race on earth then God will be left with no one to obey Him. Therefore, Satan deceived Adam and Eve to rebel against God, but the all-knowing and all-powerful God knew the remedy even before the foundation of the earth. The sin or rebellion of Adam and Eve brought a rift between God and the human race, for everyone is born a sinner. God cursed this earth or the ground with thorns due to the sin of Adam and Eve. Looking at Genesis 3:17-18 "And unto Adam he said, Because thou hearkened unto the voice of thy wife, and hast eaten of the tree, of which I commanded thee saying, Thou shalt not eat of it: cursed is the ground for thou sake; in sorrow shalt thou eat of it all the days of thou life; Thorns also and thistles shall it bring forth to thee; and thou shalt eat the herb of the field" The fall came as a result of sin, which also implement a curse on earth and thorns became the symbol for curse. Looking at Heb. 6:7-8 "For the earth which drinketh in the rain that cometh oft upon it, and bringeth forth herbs meet for them by whom it is dressed, receiveth blessing from God. But that which beareth thorns and briers is rejected, and is nigh unto cursing; whose end is to be burned." Therefore thorn is not only a symbol for curse but rejection, whose end is to be burned. Rejecting Jesus Christ in this world means such a person's sin is retained, the person is under a curse and is rejected by God, and that person is heading for the final doom to be burned in an everlasting hell fire. Sin and his twin brother curse have no place in the sight of God. God then prepared a sacrificial lamb right from the foundation of the earth to take away not only the sin of this world but also the curse which was brought upon the earth due to the rebellion of Adam and Eve against the Most High God. Blood needs to be shed for pacification and redemption of the human race. Looking at Heb. 9:22 "And almost all things are by the law purged with blood; and without shedding of blood is no remission." There is no remission of sins without the shedding of blood, therefore God prepared a sacrificial Lamb for the human race. When Adam and Eve sin against God, the Bible declares that God clothe them with coat of skins which shows that either a lamb or a cow was slaughter for God to make those clothes. Therefore, blood was shed for the sin of Adam and Eve. The Lamb that was prepared before the foundation of the world to take away sin and the curse of the earth is Jesus Christ. Looking at John 3:16 "For God so loved the world, that he gave his only begotten Son, that whosoever believeth in him should not perish, but have everlasting life." That is, the sacrificial death of Jesus Christ is to wash anyone who will believe from sins and to restore such a person into good relationship with God. The death of Jesus Christ did not only deal with the sins of humankind but also the curse of the ground or earth. The prophet Isaiah prophesied that the thorns will be replaced with a fir tree. Looking at Isaiah 55:13 "Instead of the thorn shall come up the fir tree, and instead of the brier shall come up the myrtle tree: and it shall be to the Lord for a name, for everlasting sign that shall not be cut off." The thorn, which is a curse is to be taken away and a fir tree will grow in it place. This also is going to be an everlasting sign, which shall never be cut off. This prophecy shows that Jesus will do away with the curse, which was pronounced on earth after the fall. This means those in Christ Jesus are no more under any curse since Jesus has done away with any curses. The time period is everlasting, so as long as I stay in the faith, then I am not under any curse. Therefore, before Jesus was crucified a crown of thorns was put on his head signifying they recognized Jesus as a King but the king of curses. The Jewish people knew the thorns to be curse so they decided to defame Jesus with a crown of thorns, not knowing it was the plan of God for Jesus to take away the curses of the earth. Matthew 27: 29 "And when they had platted a crown of thorns, they put it upon his head, and a reed in his right hand; and they bowed the knee before him, and mocked him, saying, Hail, King of the Jews!" Therefore, the Jewish people knew the significance of thorns being a curse and that was the reason why a crown of thorns was put on his head. In so doing, Jesus took away the curses that were upon the earth. Also according to the Old Testament Laws, anyone who is hung on the tree is a curse. Jesus has a crown of thorns and was also hang on the tree. Therefore, Jesus did not only take the curses that were upon the earth, but also the curses that were in the air or atmosphere. Looking at Gal. 3: 13 "Christ hath redeemed us from the curse of the law, being made a curse for us: for it is written, curse is every one that hangeth on a tree." The fall brought sin which, separates the humanity from God and this brought a condemnation on humanity as the relation between the Creator and the creation was broken. The fall also brought curses on humanity, which have been a major hindrance to our progress and well-being on this earth. The death of Jesus was paramount and important to deal with sin and curses, which were brought on humanity due to the fall. Jesus did not just die but raise from death. Jesus has the power to lay down his life and to take it back. One thing that differentiates Christianity from any form of religion is the rising up of Jesus from the death. There is no other religion that can claim of its leader rising up from the death. "Without the raising of Jesus from the dead, Christian preaching and Christian faith is futile (1 Cor. 15: 14-20). More than that: without the raising of Jesus from the dead the community of believers, the Church, is meaningless. Only the certainty that the crucified Christ lives on as the risen Christ, glorified by God, gives us the solution to the riddle of Jesus as a person and makes the Church possible and real [3]

Satan did not know the plan of God for humankind or he would not have crucified our Lord and Savior Jesus Christ. Satan thought if he was able to get rid of Jesus that will be the end and he (Satan) will be able to have the whole world in his hand, but that was Satan's biggest mistake. 1Cor. 2: 7-9 "But we speak the wisdom of God in a mystery, even the hidden wisdom, which God ordained before the world unto our glory. Which none of the princes of this world knew: for had they known it, they would not have crucified the Lord of glory. But as it is written, Eye hath not seen, nor ears heard, neither have entered into the heart of man, the things which God hath prepared for them that love him." This means God prepared Jesus Christ to die for the sins of humankind before creation. This is a mystery and we need the revelation of the Holy Spirit to understand it. If Satan knew that the death of Jesus would pave the way for humankind to restore a good relationship with the Father, Satan would not have crucified Jesus. This also shows that Satan is not aware of what God has in store for Christians. God has a high place for every child of God, and no matter what be the obstacle in one's life, God will let us reach our heights. It was with pride and jealousy, that made Satan to decide to overthrow God, and to exalt his throne above the stars of God, so that he would be like the Most High. The main reason for this stupidity was to get the creation of God to worship him. It is so sad that he could deceive even one third of the angels to follow his diabolical plans. Satan and his fallen angels failed to overthrow God, therefore God has prepared a place for Satan and his fallen angles and anyone who will not accept what God has done for the human race. Satan is so crafty that he was able to deceived Adam and Eve (the first human creation of God) to sin against God, therefore tarnishing, the whole human race. God, who is all- knowing and knows from the beginning to the end, has to do something amazing to redeem the human race. God sent his Son Jesus Christ to die on the cross to deliver anyone who will believe in Christ sacrificial death from the wiles of the enemy (Satan). Jesus has paid the ransom to set us free from the hands of Satan and brought us into His (Jesus) own hand as seen in; Jn 10: 27-29 "My sheep hear my voice, and I love them, and they follow me; And I give unto them eternal life; and they shall never perish, neither shall any man pluck them out of my hand. "The practical bearing of this doctrine (Jesus as a ransom paid to Satan) is that Christ died for all (2Cor. V.15.), and His death is the objective cause why all receive grace enough to resist both their own weakness and the temptations of the world and of the devil. But if theoretically one asks: "How did Christ free us from the power of the devil? What precise aspect or relation in Christ's death referred specifically to the devil, so as to overcome him and release men from his domination?" then the answer becomes disconcertingly difficult and troublesome. The Fathers of the Church picture the thing as a struggle between God and the devil for the souls of men; and in that struggle the devil's weapons are lying, deceit, hatred, calumny, instigation to violence and to murder. God's weapons are truth, justice, love, praise, meekness and humility; and God conquers in the struggle. In depicting the conflict, however, the Fathers and ecclesiastical writers sometimes use language, which has caused scandal to some who have taken it too literally; Origen, for instance, says: "We were sold to sin, He redeemed us with His own blood from him who had bought us. . . . We term ransom that money which is paid to the enemy to free the captives he holds. The human race was such a captive, having being vanquished in the conflict with sin, and taken prisoner by the devil. Christ became our ransom, that is, He delivered Himself to our enemies. He shed all His precious blood for which the devil is thirsted. The devil had bought us with special kind of currency: "His coin, the coin which bears his image upon it, is murder, adultery, thieving, and in general all forms of sin. Such is the devil's money, of which his treasury is, alas, all too full. With this money he bought us and received a deed of ownership over us"—the "Handwriting against us" of which St. Paul speaks in Colossians ii. 14, which Christ affixed to the cross. As a ransom price, the devil demanded the precious blood of Christ; God gave him this price by allowing him to kill Christ. Nevertheless, the devil deceived himself; because Christ could not be held in the realm of death, and in the rising from

5

the dead, Christ broke the power of death and the gate of hell, and make us all partakers in His resurrection.[4] Jesus Christ has promise Christians who will abide by the Word of God, that, he will come again after preparing a place in His Father's house to take the genuine Christians to be with Him in His Father's house. The works of the devil has already been destroyed, but the devil will make everything through craftiness to get many people to do his bidden. Looking at 1 John 3: 8 "He that committeth sin is of the devil; for the devil sinneth from the beginning. For this purpose the Son of God was manifested, that he might destroy the works of the devil." The major work of Satan is to get the children of God to sin against God. But Jesus has broken the power of the enemy which will cause the children of God to be rebellious and disobedient to God.

I will do my best to write about the Devil that I know from my Biblical and African traditional back ground. As a little boy, my great grandfather, my from my mother side, were all idol worshipers. One of my great uncle by name Dankese (literally meaning big house) worshiped the idol by name Tigari. My uncle was fond of me so I was so closed to him to learn a whole lot of devilish arts. My uncle would always say "you should let people fear you and let them see how powerful you are by using your powers (demonic powers) to cause havoc and panic in the society." There was a friend of my uncle who could use his demonic powers on pregnant women. This man would cast a spell on a pregnant woman so that when the woman gave birth the child would have a constant and strong convulsion, which no medical science could cure unless the child was sent to this man, who would charge exorbitantly and healed the child with his demonic powers. When the women were pregnant in my little village no one would like to see this man. He died long time ago, and many people in my little village are now Christians to worry about such devilish acts. This is exactly how the devil works, to cause havoc panic and deaths in the society so that people will be afraid, perplex, confused and will not know what to do. Satan is so cunning and crafty that he will let you put the blame on God. If God is all- powerful and all- knowing, then why all these evils in this world? I have known the works of the enemy enough, through the African Traditional Religion, to put the blame on God. There are so many evil in the world that one may think God is not all that powerful or all-knowing.

"On October 11, 1978, United Press International reported that a father kept his daughter, Tina Ann, 10, imprisoned in a 3-foot by 4-foot closet in [his small, white frame house] while he slowly beat her to death. He buried her under a dilapidated shed at the rear of the house and the family left town several months later." On January 1, 1980, UPI reported that "Thai pirates held 121 Vietnamese women and children captive on a deserted jungle island for seven days, raping them and hunting them down like animals. . . . One eight-year-old little girl was raped by 100 different men. . . . The pirates took as much pleasure in the hunt as in the capture." Evil—radical evil—exists, and its existence imposes on us the obligation of attempting to understand it and transform it."[5] Satan and his evil works can only be understood from Biblical prospective. Satan's major work is destruction, he does not know how to create but to destroy. Satan and his evil forces want to see the destruction of the human race. They will do everything to bring hardship and suffering to the human race. Thanks and glory be to God, for every child of God is protected and shield from the arsenal of the enemy. Isaiah 54:17 "No weapon that is formed against thee shall prosper; and every tongue that shall rise against thee in judgment thou shalt condemn." Our God has spoken and He is watching over His Word to perform it.

Where are Satan and his demonic forces?

According to the Bible Satan and his angels used to live in heaven, the very presence of God, until Lucifer who turned to be Satan decided to usurp power from God, so that he will be worshiped. There was a fight in heaven. Satan and his angels were defeated and cast out of heaven to this earth. Rev. 12:9 "And the great dragon was cast out, that old serpent, called the Devil, and Satan, which deceiveth the whole world: was cast out into the earth, and his angels were cast out with him". God has prepared a place for Satan and his evil spirits, which is hell but they are not confined to hell. A time is coming when God will confine Satan, his evil spirits and all the people who reject the redemption in Jesus Christ, to this place called hell, where there is eternal torment.

SATAN AND HIS FALLEN ANGELS

Satan has an enormous power which he is using to fight against Christians and the world at large. He uses his powers to hinder the prayers of the saints so that he can tarnish their faith in the Almighty God. Satan has position his forces, the fallen angels, in such a way as to fight against Christians. Satan is pleased with those who are not Christians for he can use them as he pleases and destroy them anytime he wishes. "The Devil and demons have filled the entire world in their lust to destroy it. Each individual has an evil spirit abiding in him to tempt him. The Devil and demons dwell in the lower air, where they range about on wings with incredible swiftness. Until Christ Passion, God allowed the demons to work against humanity with the limits that he had set, acting as his agents to test us and punish us. Their power was a corollary of Satan's just power over us as a result of original sin. Christ Passion has weakened and doomed the demons, placing them within our power, for we can now repel them by faith in Christ; yet they still remain free to attack us until the last judgment, and presently they still exercise wide authority in the world under God's permission. God has two purposes in allowing the Devil power over a person—to tempt and to punish."[6] Let us look at Ephesians to know how Satan has position his forces. "Finally, my brethren, be strong in the Lord, and in the power of his might. Put on the whole amour of God, that ye may be able to stand against the wiles of the devil. For we wrestle not against flesh and blood, but against *principalities,* against *powers,* against the *rulers of the darkness of this world,* against *spiritual wickedness in high places.* (Eph 6:10-13). Satan has divided his fallen angels into four battalions according to the duties assigned to them. These fallen angels are the demons, which the enemy has divided into—

- *Principalities*: These are evil spirits assigned by Satan to work within a territory or a country. Usually they work within the federal government, state, or within localities. Why do you think in Paul's epistle to Timothy, he admonished the believers to pray for those who are in authority? If we do not pray for those in authority, the devil will use them to accomplish his wish. "I exhort therefore, that, first of all, supplications, prayers, intercessions, and giving of thanks, be made for all men; For kings, and for all that are in authority; that we may lead a quiet and peaceable life in all godliness and honesty. For this is good and acceptable in the sight of God our Saviour; Who will have all men to be saved, and to come unto the knowledge of the truth. For there is one God, and one mediator between God and men, the man Christ Jesus" (1 Tm 2:1-5). If Paul is to write this letter today, he would have used the word presidents or head of state, or prime minister instead of king. We have to pray for those in authority so that we will have the right leadership and government to lead a quiet and peaceable life. If we do not want to see wars and uprising in our countries and states, then we need to pray for those in authority. The sad thing is that many Christians are not interested in politics, and this has opened many countries, states, and local politics for unbelievers who can be used by the enemy to rule with iron hands and greedily amass wealth, and put those they are suppose to serve in bondage of fear and oppression. There are so many nations around the world that their leaders have their own interest at heart rather than the interest of the people they are to serve. They become rich and make their families and friends rich at expense of the ordinary people. Let us look at the so-called Third Worlds.

The leaders of these nations can develop the transportation systems in their country, create jobs, and change educational systems that are old and outmoded. They can open more medical schools to see to the health of the ordinary people, but these leaders come in and leave the situation worse than they meet it. They eat the national cake and leave nothing for the ordinary people. The rich becomes richer and the poor poorer. Christians have to do away with the veil that is covering our eyes to see that we can enter into politics and play it neat to do away with the stigma around politics or the unbelievers will continue to play it dirty. Christians need to pray effectively for God to intervene in everyday politics and raise people who fear God into power. If we do not pray, then Satan will bring his people to be the head of government.

Christians have to pray effectively against principalities so as to get the form of government that will see to the welfare of ordinary people. "By the blessing of the upright the city is exalted; but it is overthrown by the mouth of the wicked" (Prov 11:11). Our cities are going to be overthrown if the righteous people are not going to enter into the local, state, and federal politics. We always pray for our needs, forgetting about politics. The effective policies of the political leaders will help to bring peace and sanity in a country, state, or city.

Let us pray effectively for our political leaders.

- *Powers*: These demons are assigned to bring in sickness, diseases, especially those that cannot be cure. They are assigned to discover and bring in incurable diseases to destroy the human population. They are assigned to see to narcotic drugs, guns, and organized crime to gain roots in our society just to bring fear and distress in the community. They do their best to entangle the society with poverty, sickness, and depression. They will not only keep you poor but also in debt. You cannot even pay your bills, and if you do not take care, they will make you homeless. These demons are powerful, and Christians need to effectively pray against the works of these powerful demons, to restore health and sanity in our communities. Satan and his forces will make things that are nasty and horrible to be perfect and good for the society. For instance, we all know that cigarette smoking is detrimental to our health, but the enemy will make smoking to be for the youth, strong, and well-known people. We will spend money to buy something that in the long run will give us cancer. I met a man in Philadelphia who asked me whether I was a smoker. I told him I do not smoke. He said, "That is good for you for I smoke from the age of fourteen, and I am now sixty-seven and have got a lung cancer from smoking. I have stop smoking, but it is too late." Why do we destroy our own bodies? The only thing that can withstand the wiles of Satan and his demonic forces is praying effectively against the works of the enemy. As Christians, we need to take the Word of God seriously and live by the Word for Satan is roaring like a l ion looking for someone to devour. Fellow Christians, let me tell you that we have a lot of prayers to do. Let us pray and stop rumor mongering and backbiting.

- *Rulers of the darkness of this world*: These demons are assigned for the night and work tediously to bring havoc to the society.

They operate in the form of wizards, witchcraft, sorceress, necromancy, voodoo, and many other forms. I met a man in a village in Ghana who told me that "the most powerful agents of Satan are those who are able to operate in the day time." He told me that he could turn into a dangerous snake, like a black cobra, during the day time and bite any person he wants to kill, and that will be the end of the person. This brings to light Psalm 91:1-8, "He that dwelleth in the secret place of the most High shall abide under the shadow of the Almighty. I will say of the Lord, He is my refuge and my fortress: my God; in him will I trust. Surely he shall deliver thee from the snare of the fowler and from the noisome pestilence. He shall cover thee with his feathers, and under his wings shalt thou trust; his truth shall be thy shield and buckler. Thou shalt not be afraid for the terror by night; nor for the arrow that flieth by day; Nor for the pestilence that walketh in darkness; nor for the destruction that wasteth at noonday. A thousand shall fall at thy side, and ten thousand at thy right hand; but it shall not come nigh thee." In Christ Jesus, we will not be afraid of the terror that comes in the night, that is, the time the forces of darkness come together to work out their diabolic plans. We will be protected from the destruction, which the enemy and his forces lash out during the noon time (the daytime). I want you to understand that witchcraft and the work of darkness are not superstition but real. It is the power of God that delivers the believer from the works of the enemy.

- *Spiritual wickedness in high places*: These spiritual wicked demons main assignment is to hinder the prayers of believers. They able to wreck the faith of many Christians, because they do not see their prayers being answered. Please do not let your faith dwindle and continue to walk according to the Word, for at the right time you are going to witness a divine power that is going to intervene on your behalf to give you answered prayers. Daniel's prayer was hindered for almost three weeks by the spiritual wickedness in high places. "Then said he unto me, Fear not, Daniel; for the first day that thou didst set thine heart to understand, and to chasten thyself before thy God, thy words were heard, and I am come for thy words. But the kingdom of Persia withstood me one and twenty days: but, lo, Michael, one of the chief princes, came to help me; and I remained there with the kings of Persia. Now I am come to make thee understand what shall befall thy people in the latter days; for yet the vision is for many days" (Dn 10:12-14). If the prayer of Daniel was hindered, then note that the prayer of every believer can also be hindered.

We need to pray constantly against these spiritual forces which Satan has assigned to hinder our prayers. They never go on holidays, they are constantly working to hinder our prayers so we should not cease in praying against their works. Daniel wanted to know and understand the times concerning his people, the children of Israel, so he started fasting and praying, but his prayer was hindered. Finally, God was able to give him the answer. I have witnessed so many hindrances to many of my prayers, but I patiently wait on God who will finally show His powers and answer my prayers. When I started praying for God to assist me to come to America for further studies, it took more than three years for the prayers to be answered. In America, I prayed with my kids more than eight years before the immigration approved and issued green cards to us. There are many things I am still praying for, and I do not give up until I see my prayer is answered. I believe so far as I do my best to walk worthy of the vocation of my calling. I believe my prayers will be answered at the right time. Satan has given a second assignment to these demons, and that is, to work against the cosmic order to bring in havoc, devastation, and destruction to humankind. They are demons assigned to the weather, the atmosphere, sea, and rivers to bring famine, draught, and very bad weather. According to the name, these demons are very wicked, and they are in high places, which is the heavenly. They can cause very bad hurricanes, tsunamis, earthquakes, and torrential rains to bring in disaster to the human race. These wicked spirits are able to cause earthquake and tsunami, like the one which happened on December 26, 2004 that devastated the Indian Ocean coastline, killing 230,000 people. These are some of the destruction, which can be caused by Satan and his wicked spirits. These wicked spirits also work through the small rivers and streams. There is a small stream in the Ashanti Region in Ghana called Antoa Nyama, and if someone is cursed by this small stream, no matter what is done if the person is at fault that person will surely died. While in high school, a friend of mine was cursed by this small stream, and he died. This friend of mine made a young lady pregnant, and he denied it. The lady called upon the name of Antoa Nyama to be a judge between them. Within three days, the stomach of my friend started swollen, and he was rushed to the hospital, but nothing could be done to save my friend. I have seen three people died because all of them were cursed by this small stream. You may take this to be superstition, but I am writing this to let you know it is true. What I want you to know is that if you are child of God and you are walking worthy of the vocation of your calling, then Antoa Nyama has no portion in your life. I was really afraid of Antoa Nyama until the day I met Jesus Christ. Jesus delivered me from the fear of AntoaNyama. "Forasmuch then as the children are partakers of flesh and blood, he also himself likewise took part of the same; that through death he might destroy him that had the power of death, that is, the devil; And deliver them who through fear of death were all their lifetime subject to bondage" (Heb 2:14-15). I was subject to bondage for the fear of death. I was really afraid of AntoaNyama, but Jesus Christ delivered me from this fear. Jesus came in the flesh and blood like any human being so that he would die to destroy the devil who has the power of death. In doing that, Jesus has released all who will believe in Him from the fear of death. I was subject to bondage for fear of death, but I am no more afraid of Antoa Nyama for Jesus Christ has delivered me from the fear of death and the wicked spirits operating through Antoa Nyama. Satan and his forces work through lust, enticement, deceptions, and fabricated lies to bring a whole community in fear and bondage. Many people think if they are rich and they are using their worth to help the poor, then they are bound for heaven. That is a big lie from the enemy. It is good to help the poor, but the only thing that set us bound for heaven is to know Jesus as our personal Savior and Lord. It is the Blood of Jesus that can break and set people free from the works of Satan. We need to pray against Satan and his forces all the time for they are working twenty-four hours a day, seven days a week, and throughout the year. They do not rest, so we should not cease in praying against the works of the enemy.[7]

Satan is very wise, cunning and crafty so we need to be Children of God who abide by the Word of God to overcome the wiles and the schemes of the enemy. It is very difficult to write about all his diabolical plans and activities around the world. I hope to do my best to write as much as I can to reveal the sinister activities of Satan. I was once listening to a testimony of a lady from South Africa who was delivered from Satan and his demonic forces. This lady was addicted to eating soil, paper, maize meal, and eraser. It took about 45 minutes for the man of God to pray and deliver this lady from the dominion of Satan and his forces. The man of God asked the spirits that had taken control of the lady, when and how did they take control of the lady? The forces of darkness replied that they were three that had taken control over her and it was since birth. These three forces of darkness were; Satan, Leviathan and Numeral, and those three act like the trinity for Satanic kingdom. In the Satanic kingdom, Satan is the father. Looking at John 8:44 "Ye are of your father the devil, and the lust of your father ye will do. He was a murderer from the beginning, and abode not in the truth, because there is no truth in him. When he speaketh a lie, he speaketh of his own: for he is a lair, and the father of it." Jesus really knew who Satan was. Satan was the devil, murderer, a liar and father of lies. Satan has built his kingdom on deception, corruption, intimidation and lies. Satan is the father and the master architect of his kingdom. Leviathan is the second in command to Satan, among the triple Satanic forces and his powerful demonic force. He is second to Satan, and exercise all the authority of Satan. Leviathan exercise all the power assigned to him in the sea, rivers and all the waters surrounding the world and the atmosphere. Looking at Isaiah 27:1 "In that day the Lord with his sore and great and strong sword shall punish leviathan the piercing serpent, even leviathan that crooked serpent; and he shall slay the dragon that is in the sea." Isaiah the prophet talks of Leviathan as the serpent and dragon, which are name given to Satan. Isaiah let us know that Leviathan is in the sea, which means he rules the sea. Simply put Leviathan is Satan who has dominion, control and doing all the diabolical evil acts in the sea. He works not only in the sea but in the rivers and streams around the world. The Leviathan is able to cause tsunami, typhoon and great storms in the ocean destroying anything in its path. An example is the powerful typhoon that killed an estimated 10,000 people and displaced more than 600,000 in central Philippines city of Tacloban in November 10, 2013. This is the hand of Satan, as his major work is to steal, kill, and destroy. The third part of this Satanic kingdom is the Numeral. This is the satanic force assign to take care of numbers, figures, digits, symbols letters or alphabets and secret messages and codes. This force of darkness uses statistics, social security numbers, codes and secret messages to work out his heinous and evil crime. In the tribulation period, Satan is going to use Numeral to bring great havoc and tribulation on earth. Rev. 13:16-18 "And he causeth all, both small and great, rich and poor, free and bond, to receive a mark in their right hand, or in their foreheads: And that no man might buy or sell, save he that had the mark, or the name of the beast, or the number of his name. Here is wisdom. Let him that hath understanding count the number of the beast: for it is the number of a man; and his number is Six hundred threescore and six (666). The Word of God clearly states that Jesus Christ is coming again for the second time. According to the Word of God, the Second Coming of Jesus Christ will be proceeded by the Rapture. The word Rapture cannot be found in the Bible but Bible Scholars coined it to mean a state of being transported into the sky to meet with the Lord Jesus Christ, which can only be done by the power of the Holy Spirit. Thorough studies shows that Rapture will happen before the Second Coming of Jesus Christ. During the Rapture, only those who are Christians who are abiding by the Word of God (that is Christians who are walking worthy of the vocation of their calling) are going to hear the Sound of the Archangel and be Rapture. During the Rapture, Jesus is coming for those who abide by His word. I want you to understand that many so called Christians are going to be left behind. If we do not obey every word of God, we can be left behind. I will be sure to obey every Word of God so that I will not be left behind. The following so called Christians are going to be left behind:

a. Lukewarm Christians; Rev. 3:14-20 (those who are rich and proud, those with half-heartedness, and self-righteousness, or simply one foot in the church and the other foot in the world).

b. Those who are not abiding by the word of God; Matt. 7:21-27 (Note that it is not the signs and wonders or the miracles that follow us, for the gifts and calling of God are without repentance; but living according to the Word of God). An example; God hates divorce so if you divorce you are not abiding by the Word. Divorce is a ploy that the devil is using to let many Christians to be left behind.

c. Christians who hate other Christians (brothers and sisters) 1 John 4: 20-21; 1 John 3: 15-18) Some Christians tend to hate the Pastor because, they are not living worthy of the vocation of their calling so anytime the Pastor preaches on anything they do not like to hear, then they tend to hate the Pastor.

d. Christians who love the world. 1 John 2: 15-18, Carnality, and worldliness.

e. Unbelievers: These are the people who do not believe in the Lord Jesus Christ. John 3: 18-19

These people are not going to be Rapture. On the last day, only Christians who are true believers, or abiding by the Word of God are going to be Rapture. This is the study of end time, which is termed the eschatology in the Seminaries and higher school of learning. After the Rapture comes in the Great Tribulation and this is the time when "The abomination of the desolation spoken of by Daniel the prophet will be revealed, Matt. 24: 15, Dan. 7:25; Dan. 9:27, which is the falling away spoken of in 2 Thess. 2: 3 "Let no man deceive you by any means: for that day shall not come, except there come a falling away first, and that man of sin be revealed, the son of perdition;" – he is the son of perdition, man of sin, the Wicked.

This mark the beginning of Great Tribulation, which has never been seen, since the beginning of the world. Matt. 24:16-26.

Great Tribulation: What is going to happen during the tribulation?

1. The man of sin, the son of perdition, the Wicked, the Antichrist will first be revealed.

2. Revelation is a difficult book but I will do my best to explain to the best of my ability with the help of the Holy Spirit.

3. In Rev 6, where the first six seals are broken (there are seven seals) and opened by the Lamb (Jesus) shows exactly the signs that Jesus talk about that will come before his Second Coming.

4. Seal 1—The Conqueror sitting upon a White horse—This signify the Rapture where Jesus will come as a Conqueror to transport those who live a righteous live in Christ.

5. Seal 2— Red horse with one sitting upon given power to take peace away from the earth and to bring war.

6. Seal 3— Black horse with one sitting on it with balance in hand to bring famine on earth.

7. Seal 4— <u>Pale</u> horse sitting on it is Death and Hell their aim is to kill with sword, hunger and death.

8. Seal 5—Shows souls of those who were slain for the Word of God, and the testimony which they held. Christians who were not rapture but stood firm for the Word of God and were slain for their testimony.

9. Rev.13 also talks about what will happen during this great tribulation. The abomination of the desolation spoken of by Daniel the prophet will be revealed, Matt. 24: 15, Dan. 7:25; Dan. 9:27, which is the falling away spoken of in 2 Thess. 2: 3 "Let no man deceive you by any means: for that day shall not come, except there come a falling away first, and that man of sin be revealed, the son of perdition;" – he is the son of perdition, man of sin, the Wicked.

10. Rev. 13: 1-7—Satan (the dragon) will give power, his seat, and great authority to the beast with blasphemy written on his forehead who would deceive everyone to worship the devil (Satan). He make war with the saints (those who were not rapture and stood firm on their grounds). For 42 months this hideous monster will torment the earth.

11. Rev. 13:11 — Another beast will come make and do all sorts of miracles. He will make an image of the first beast and make this image to speak and cause that as many that will not worship the image of the beast should be killed.

12. This is the period of great tribulation and the whole tribulation may take about 7 years.

13. Rev.13:16-18 "And causeth all, both small and great, rich and poor, free and bond, to receive a mark in their right hand, or in their foreheads: and that no man might buy or sell, save he that had the mark or the name of the beast, or the number of his name. Here is wisdom. Let him that hath understanding count the number of the beast: for it is the number of a man; and his number is Six hundred three score and six (666).

The Second Coming of Jesus Christ:

1. Seal 6— Great earthquake, sun become black, moon as blood, and the stars of heaven fall. Matt. 24: 27. This will happen just before the Second Coming of Jesus.

2. Follow by the great day of his wrath—That is the judgment.

Matt. 24: 27 "For as the lightning cometh out of the east, and shineth even unto the west; so shall also the coming of the Son of man be. Matt. 24: 29-31 "Immediately after the tribulation of those days shall the sun be darkened, and the moon shall not give her light, and the stars shall fall from heavens shall be shaken: And shall appear the sign of the Son of man in heaven: and shall all the tribes of the earth mourn, and they shall see the Son of man coming in the clouds of heaven with power and great glory. And he shall send his angels with a great sound of a trumpet, and they shall gather together his elect from the four winds, from one end of heaven to the other." After the Tribulation, then comes the Second Coming of Christ.

Note that the major assignment of Satan and his forces is to work and get you denied your faith in God. They worked 24 hrs a day, and seven days a week to frustrate Christians and dwindle their faith in the Almighty God. Their main target is the Pastor, especially if you are not walking worthy of the vocation of your calling. They tend to destroy Christian marriages especially the Pastors' marriage. Getting Pastors involve in extra-marital affairs, and squandering of church funds.

Chapter Two

The Battle ground

Satan and his demonic force are waging a war against humanity and like every battle, there is a place where the battle is fought. The battle field is the mind. Looking at 2 Corinthians 10: 3-5 "For though we walk in the flesh, we do not war after the flesh: [For the weapons of our warfare are not carnal, but mighty through God to the pulling down of strong holds;] Casting down imaginations, and every high thing that exalteth itself against the knowledge of God, and bringing into captivity every thought to the obedience of Christ;" It is clearly stated that we do not war after the flesh, which means it is not a physical battle. This warfare is a spiritual warfare, which is being wage by Satan and his demonic forces every micro- second around the clock, all year around. They take no recess, break, or leave, it is a continuous warfare. The battle field is the mind. That is why it is important to bring any though under the obedience of Christ. This means allowing the Word of God to take control of your mind or thinking. How do we do this? Study the Word of God daily and applying what we have studied in everyday life. We also have to cast out from our minds any thoughts that do not confirm to the Word of God. No one can do it for you, you have to do it yourself. There is no need for us to fight against the people who we think are the cause of our problems. This is because, we do not war after the flesh. It is a spiritual warfare and the weapons of our warfare are mighty, for it is God who is fighting this battle for us, but we need to hand the battle over to Him through prayers. We should not forget to cast down any thoughts or imagination that do not conform with the Word of God. That is why we need to study Word to know any thought that is not in line with the Word. Example, let say there is a beautiful lady in the church who is not married. You are a man who is not married and finds this lady attractive and wants not only to date her but have sexual intercourse with her. If set thought comes into your mind, then you have to cast it out, for having sex before marriage is fornication and the Bible is against it. It is right to talk about dating the girl but let it be under the guidance of your Pastor or women's leader. If you are married, then stay with your partner and do not think of any other person. Another example is rumor and backbiting, if you know you cannot substantiate with facts what you are saying about your friend or church member then stop it. Can you say it if the person you are talking about is around? If you cannot, then stop it. Rumor and backbiting is killing the church and friendship. Do you think someone will just pick a gun kill love ones, for instance, wife and children? What happens in the spirit world if not check will be manifested in the flesh. The devil will bring thought of depression, pain from what someone has done to you and then give you the thought of killing the person. If you are not a child of God, then you cannot control what Satan and his force will bring to you and you will go and do the bidding of Satan. Let me tell you, every year, Satan and his forces need the blood of human to drink, for libation and to empower their might, especially, the fetish priest, the voodoo priest and the necromancer, to be more powerful in their work for the devil. They are able to accomplish this through, gun violence, car accidents, abortion, fighting among the nations and many other things. Satan and his force can also bring in a bad weather to kill so many people to get the blood needed for their work. They can also bring in an incurable disease, like ebola to kill so many people to get the blood that they need. Satan is so cunning and crafty, and has plans only to steal, kill and destroy. We need to be aware of the devil, his might, and schemes in order to be able to fight a winning battle against the devil. The Bible tells us so many ways that we as Christians can fight this battle; first, we need to have a good knowledge of the Word of God and believe in what we know. Looking at Hosea 4: 6 "My people are destroyed for lack of knowledge: because thou hast rejected knowledge, I will also reject thee," If we reject knowledge, God is also going to reject us and it will be terrible for us to be left at the mercy of Satan and his demonic forces. We will be fighting a losing battle. We have to get a good knowledge of God and His word, but this knowledge should not be a head knowledge, for it should be a knowledge that is transferred to the heart, that is believing in this knowledge. Looking at Psalm 119: 11 "Thy word have I hid in my heart, that I might not sin against thee." As soon as the head knowledge becomes a heart knowledge, it is difficult to sin against God. Secondly, we need to renew our mind. We have to renew our mind with the Word of God. That is we have to study the Word of God, and let what we study take control of our mind set. We think about what we have study and put it into practice in our everyday life. Looking Romans 12: 1-2 "I Beseech you therefore, brethren, by the mercies of God, that ye present your bodies a living sacrifice, holy, acceptable unto God, which is your reasonable service. And be not conformed to this world: but be ye transformed by the renewing of your mind, that ye may prove what is that good, and acceptable, and perfect, will of God." When we renew our mind, then we tend to live according to the Word of God, and the old ways which, we used to live our lives would be done away. When we renew our mind, many things changes. For example when I become a Christian, the way I used to dress changed as I renew my mind with the word of God. At first I dressed to attract attention of the women, when I was going to a disco, I will make sure, my dressing will be out of the ordinary. Now I dress nicely for Christ. The music I listened to changed. Now I, do not listen to any music unless it is a gospel music. I always need something to edify my spirit that is the reason I do not listen to any trash music. Thirdly, we need to put on the whole armor of God, for when we put on the armor of God, then we can fight Satan and his forces and win the battle. Looking at Eph 6:11-18 "Put on the whole armour of God, that ye may be able to stand against the wiles of the devil. For we wrestle not against flesh and blood, but against principalities, against powers, against rulers of the darkness of this world, against spiritual wickedness in high places. Wherefore take unto you the whole armour of God, that ye may be able to withstand in the evil day, and having done all, to stand. Stand therefore, having your loins girt about with truth, and having on the breastplate of righteousness; And your feet shod with the preparation of the gospel of peace; Above all, taking the shield of faith, wherewith ye shall be able to quench all the fiery darts of the wicked. And take the helmet of salvation, and the sword of the Spirit, which is the word of God. Praying always with all prayer and supplication in the Spirit, and watching thereunto with all perseverance and supplication for all saints;" This is a description of the armory of a Roman Soldier. The Christians at that time knew how the Roman soldiers dresses for battle so it was easy for Paul to use the picture of the Roman Soldier. Satan has a formidable force to fight humankind, especially Christians. Satan has declared a war against any child of God, so we have to stand firm in the armor of God to fight a winning battle. The first armor is truth, that is having our loins girt about with truth. This means truth is the belt for our battle outfit. If our belt is torn then our battle outfit cannot stand and we will be fighting a losing battle. What is truth? The Free Merriam- Webster Dictionary defines truth as the real facts about something; the things that are true. The quality or state of being true. Truth is something the enemy cannot stand. Looking at John 8:32 "And ye shall know the truth, and the truth shall make you free." Truth is one of the biggest weapon to fight Satan and his forces. Satan has been able to build this world systems on lies, deceit, cheating and intimidation. I know someone with MBA-Finance but could not secure job for the mere fact that this person has a credit card debt. If this person go for interview and says I have a credit card debt then that is the end. This person says they will find out if I do not tell them for they are going to do a credit check. This person who was telling the truth end up working with a home care job taking care of old people. In so many places one has to lie either to get a job, and a lot of immigrants to get their stay. If you stand for the truth it may be difficult but in the end you will win. It is easy to tell lies but if you do not take care, it will become part of your life and all the time you will be telling lies. If we are prepared to fight the enemy then we should be prepared to tell the truth, no matter what be the cost. The next armour is the breastplate of righteousness. We have truth, which is the belt, that is holding all our battle attire in place, then comes righteousness which is the breastplate. When the breastplate is not strong then the enemy can easily shot his dart straight to your heart. What is righteousness? Dictionary.com defines righteousness as the quality or state of being just or rightful. In Christianity, this means your moral life is right with God. One has to accept Jesus as his/her personal Savior and Lord to be righteous before God. It is the Blood of Jesus Christ that has washed us, purified us and given us right standing before God. Looking at 2 Cor 5:20-21 "Now then we are ambassadors for Christ, as though God did beseech you by us: we pray you in Christ's stead, be ye reconciled to God. For he hath made him to be sin for us, who knew no sin; that we might be made the righteousness of God in him." God made Christ Jesus to take away the sins of the world to the cross, so that anyone who believes in the sacrificial death of Christ will be wash of his/her sin. Then such a person is reconciled to God, and the righteousness of God is imputed to him/her and that person also becomes an ambassador in this world for Christ. The righteousness of God has been imputed to us as Christians, and the only thing that can soil this righteousness is sin. Sin is simply disobeying God or being rebellious against God and His word. We should know that we have the armour of God to fight the enemy. Non-Christians have no armour and the enemy or Satan can kill them at anytime and in any place. I learned there was a Ghanaian who was living in New York, and had been able to build a beautiful house in Ghana. The house was occupied by his family and when he went on holidays he found that the house was so dirty and not kept in good shape, so he reprimanded the elders of the family. These elders got annoyed and one told him, you will never get back to New York again. On his way to New York, this man had a heart attack and died in the plane, so his dead body was dropped in France. If you are not a Christian, you will never go scot free if Satan and his demonic forces got angry at you. Let me tell you, you are at the mercy of the wizards, witches, sorcerers, voodoos, necromancers, diviners, and all the demonic forces that are bidding the works of Satan. Aside from truth, and righteousness, the next armour is that, one's feet should be cover with the preparation of the gospel of peace. This mean the gospel of peace should be your foot-wear. We know that we cannot go to any place without our foot-wear. This means as Christians wherever we go, even if there is a rift, fighting and misunderstanding, we should bring the gospel of peace. Peace is something that Satan cannot stand. Satan is always comfortable with war, misunderstanding, backbiting, and hooliganism. What then is peace? The Wikipedia, the free encyclopedia defines peace as an occurrence of harmony characterized by lack of violence, conflict behaviors and the freedom from fear of violence. When there is peace there is no fear of intimidation and violence. Looking at Rom 5:1 "Therefore being justified by faith, we have peace with God through our Lord Jesus Christ." This means it only through Jesus that we can have peace with God. This peace is a heavenly peace. It is the peace that come from the throne of God. Looking at Joh 14:27 "Peace I leave with you, my peace I give unto you; not as the world giveth, give I unto you. Let not your heart be trouble, neither let be afraid." Jesus said my peace I give unto you. This shows there are two kinds of peace. The peace that comes from heaven and the peace that comes from the earth. The heavenly peace is from God and the earthly peace is man-made. You become a peace maker if you allow the gospel of peace to be your foot wear. Satan is the master architect for confusion, misunderstanding and war, therefore we as children of God has to confront these forces, with the gospel of peace. The sad thing is Satan has been able to turn most churches into war zones, with rumors, backbiting, gossiping, fear and intimidation. We should be the children of peace, and proclaimed this peace wherever we are or go. As we proclaim the gospel of peace, then Satan and his force are intimidated as they see most of their work been destroyed. Let us be the children of God. Looking at Matt. 5:9 "Blessed are the peacemakers: for they shall be called the children of God." Let us work hard to bring peace wherever we are, and we will be fighting a winning battle against the forces of darkness. The next armor is the shield of faith, wherewith ye shall be able to quench all the fiery darts of the wicked. Paul was describing a Roman soldier the armor he puts on to fight any battle. The Roman soldier has a shield, which he uses for defense. If it is the present day then, Paul will say, faith should be the missile defense system of our battle with the devil. The devil is afraid of the small faith that a child of God has for with a little faith, miracles are done and most of the works of the enemy are destroyed. Looking at Luke 17:6 "And the Lord said, if ye had faith as a grain of a mustard seed, ye might say unto this sycamine tree, be thou plucked up by the root, and be thou planted in the sea; and it should obey you." Therefore with a little faith, a miracle can be born. Satan knows this so the devil will find ways a means to dwindle the faith of the child of God. How then can we build our faith? Looking at Rom 10:17 "So then faith cometh by hearing and hearing by the word of God." Note that whatever you hear can give you faith. This faith can be positive faith if what you are hearing is from the word of God and negative faith or unbelief if what you are hearing is not from the word of God. For example, if a believer is sick and listen to the fact from the doctor, the believer's faith in the healing power of God may dwindle. But if this believer starts to move by faith in the Word of God and start confessing that by the stripes which Jesus received he/she is healed then such a believer is going to be healed. For we walk by faith and not by sight. We need to build our faith for our prayers to be answered. Faith is gained by reading the Word of God, believing in what we read and living our live according to what we read. We have to read the Word of God daily in order to build our faith. If we do not put what we read into practice, then that faith is dead. Looking at Heb 11:6 "But without faith it is impossible to please him: for he that cometh to God must believe that he is, and that he is a rewarder of them that diligently seek him." It is a daily affair and not a Sunday church going affair. Abraham became the friend of God because, first he learned to hear from God and secondly he believed in what God told him and thirdly he put what he heard from God into practice. God told Abraham to leave his father's house and go to an unknown place. Abraham was comfortable with his father's house but he left his comfort zone and left to the unknown. God blessed Abraham because Abraham believed in God. If we are the children of Abraham then we should be prepared to step into the unknown trusting God to lead us. The next armor is the helmet of salvation; it is important to know that you are saved by the precious blood of the savior Jesus Christ. This salvation is your helmet and you should wear it all the time. If you have your helmet on, the enemy may throw a spiritual arrow against your head but you will be able to stand if you have the helmet of salvation and you will not suffer any casualty. The last armor is the sword of the spirit, which is the Word of God.

Chapter Three

Fear

If there be any virtue in not being an infidel, the devil may claim this virtue. If it be any praise to be always busy, the devil may claim that praise, for he is always busy and very busy. But his character does not spring from his faith. His faith makes him tremble; his character makes him the devil.

The devil is a very busy character. He does a big business, but he does it well, that is, as well as a mean business can be done. He has large experience, big brains, a black heart, great force, and tireless industry, and is of great influence and great character. All his immerse resources and powers are laid out for evil. Only evil inspires his activities and energies.[8] Satan and his forces are working 24 hr a day, 7 days a week, 4 weeks a month, and 12 month a year. Simply put they work 365 days a year without vacation. They have no time off, recreation or leave. They work every second and every minute of the clock. I will do my best to expose the works of the enemy, using the Word of God. The following are some of works of the enemy. Fear and intimidation are the major weapons of the enemy. Looking at Prov. 1:27 "When your fear cometh as desolation, and your destruction cometh as a whirlwind; when distress and anguish cometh upon you." If we reject the instruction of the Lord or the word of God, then the Word of God says, there is a time that fear will come upon us. It will come with desolation and destruction. Not only that but distress and anguish. Fear is one of the weapon of the enemy.

1. **Fear:** Looking at 2Tim1:7 "For God hath not given us the spirit of fear; but of power, and of love, and of a sound mind." Fear is a major weapon of the enemy. What is fear? Fear is a state of weird feeling or unpleasant feeling caused by the possibility of danger or threat. The Word of God says there is a spirit behind fear. This spirit is not from God, then, it is an evil spirit from the camp of the enemy. There is a powerful force behind fear to keep people in servitude and bondage of terror. There are so many things in the world, which,

the devil can use to cause fear. Therefore, we have to put risk in so many things that we do. What then is risk? Risk is a state of mind, knowing the possibility of danger or threat but preparing oneself to take a stake in or chance in the incident. In Christianity, faith in God is what is used to overcome fear and to take a risk. Let me give you an example; for instance, no one finds a partner to get married with the intention of divorcing the partner later in life. The Word of God says "I hate divorce." If God hates divorce then the devil loves to see divorce. Therefore, married Christians have to establish their married on the Word of God to avoid divorce. Faith is simply believing and living your life according to the Word of God. I will now do my best to state some of the causes of fear:

- **Fear of death:** Everyone seems to be afraid of dying. We want to look young, energetic, strong and good looking, and never grow old. We have to face the fact that, everyone will grow old, weak and one day die. Looking at Heb. 2: 14-15 "Forasmuch then as the children are partakers of flesh and blood, he also himself likewise took part of the same; that through death he might destroy him that had the power of death, that is, the devil; And deliver them who through fear of death were all their lifetime subject to bondage." Jesus Christ became a partaker of flesh and blood, so that through his death on the cross, he might destroy the devil's power over death. Jesus did not only destroy the devil's power over death but he also delivered us who were subject to bondage, because of the fear of death from the enemy. I remember, when I was young, my senior sister sent me to a fetish shrine where the fetish priest made some cuts with a sharp knife on my forehead, the back of my head and my back and he put some black powered substance in the cuts to make me invisible from the witches in my family so that they could not kill me. I went through this ordeal because I was afraid to die. When I got to high school, there was no other shrine that I was afraid of than the shrine of Antoa Nyama. Three people that I knew of were killed by this Antoa Nyama so I did not want to hear that name. When I became a Christian in August 1984 and found out that Jesus Christ had delivered me from the fear of death and all satanic forces, including that of Antoa Nyama, I was so happy. I know where I will be going, when I die, so I am not afraid to die. I am going to be with my Lord. Fear is a terrible thing to get hold of anyone, so do not allow fear to grip you. If you do not know Jesus then you need to give your life to Jesus. In Africa many people are in bondage and fear due to idol worshiping. There is a city in the Volta Region of Ghana called Kete-Krachi, which is known for its terrible and notorious idol shrine known as Denteh. One of the ministers of the Apostolic Church in Ghana, Apostle Samuel Awidi served as a District Pastor in this area for eight years and in his book he writes "Dominant on the religious scene were the African traditional religions who demonstrated their power openly. Strange and tragic events and deaths were attributed to the wrath of gods of these shrines, including the voodoo, and Denteh shrines. Rampant among these mysterious events were death by thunderstorms and lightning, drowning in the Volta Lake and poisonous snake bites among others. The shrines were quick to identify or determine the causes of these and other tragic events. Several natives of Krachi and sojourners became victims or potential victims to these mysterious and tragic events in the Kete-Krachi District. Occasionally, they have to pacify the gods of these shrines who appear to have control over their fate to avoid being victims of plague. Some went to the extent of serving as slaves at the shrine as a requirement to save their lives. It was during this period of religious slavery and chaos that the church came boldly, with the formation of a branch of the Ghana Pentecostal and Charismatic Council, (CPCC) to publicly spread the gospel of Jesus Christ with regular crusades all over the town and its environs. The Church's banner captured themes such as "Jesus came to set the captives free," "Jesus died for our sins that we might live," "Jesus Christ is the answer;" Salvation comes from Christ alone."[9]

- **Fear of evil disaster:** There are people out there, who all the time thinking that, something terrible bad is going to happen to them. Looking at Job 1:4-5 "And his sons went and feasted in their houses, every one his day; and sent and called for their sisters to eat and to drink with them. And it was so, when the days of their feasting were gone about, that Job sent and sanctified them, and rose up early in the morning, and offered burnt offerings according to the number of them all: for Job said, It may be that my sons have sinned, and cursed God in their hearts. Thus did Job continually." Children will be children, no matter what. Job's children were the party type, so they were all the time feasting, partying and may be dancing. Job was so much afraid that his children might sin against God. Job had to sanctify and offer burnt offering for everyone after every party that these children would throw. Fear of evil disaster gives conception of evil and if not check, this conception will give birth to evil disaster. This is what happened in the case of Job. The children were having a party, when a strong wind (like a hurricane) came in, and the building in which they were having the party, could not stand the wind but collapsed and fell and killed Job's children. Let us look at what Job said in Job 3:25 "For the thing which I greatly feared is come upon me, and that which I was afraid of is come unto me." We should not be afraid of something evil coming to us or our children or family. When you are afraid, just pray and lay your burden at the cross and Jesus will give you rest. Jesus said in Mat 11: 28 "Come unto me, all ye that labour and are heavy laden, and I will give you rest." Fear of evil disaster happening to you is a heavy laden which need to be thrown at the cross. God has promised to be with us, so we should not entertain fear of evil disaster in our lives. Ps 23: 4 "Yea, though I walk through the valley of the shadow of death, I will fear no evil: for thou art with me; thy rod and thy staff they comfort me. Even in the face of evil we should not be afraid of evil, for Lord Jesus will never forsake us.

- **Fear of the future:** Many people are afraid of what tomorrow holds for them. People are worried about the stock market, global warming, sky rocketing tuitions for the university education, mortgage, marriages, and safety and welfare of our kids, just to mention a few. These things are very important but we have no power or strength to control them. As Christians we need to hand everything over to the Lord Jesus. We can go through this horrific world with the peace of God. Rom 5:1 "Therefore being justified by faith, we have peace with God through our Lord Jesus Christ". Justify means to validate; that is the heavenly court has defended us from any accusation that the enemy brought against us. This means our faith in Jesus Christ has defended us from any past, present and future accusations of the enemy. We need to live according to the Word of God so that the enemy will not get anything against us. We should not be afraid of the future for our God holds the future in his hands. Let us look at Jer 29:11-13 "For I know the thoughts that I think toward you, saith the Lord, thought of peace, and not of evil, to give you an expected end. Then shall ye call upon me, and ye shall go and pray unto me, and I will hearken unto you. And ye shall seek me, and find me, when ye shall search for me with all your heart." We need to seek the Lord with all our heart, a total surrender of our will, spirit, soul and body to the Lord Jesus Christ. The Lord does not need half of your heart, He needs the whole heart. When we are sold out to the Lord then we need not be afraid of what the future holds in store for us. Our Heavenly Father who holds the future in His hands has a plan for our lives. He will make our feet like that of the deer and will let us reach our heights. God will help us through this life as we continue to trust on him. We have hope in this world and in the world to come. Let us look at 1Cor. 15:19 "If in this life only we have hope in Christ, we are of all men most miserable." We do not look at the situation or the circumstance but we are moved by the Word of God. Our Father has a plan for our future and He has the power to bring it to pass.

- **Fear of failure:** There are people who are afraid that the business they have started are not going to work. The business will fail because you have no hope in what you have started. Job said in Job 3: 25 "For the thing which I greatly feared is come upon me, and which I was afraid of is come unto me." If you are afraid your marriage is not going to work then it will break because you are calling in for divorce for your marriage. As Christians we do not have to entertain fear. When fear comes in to grip us let us lay it at the feet of the cross. Let us remember that God has not given us the spirit of fear. Fear is from the devil so do not allow fear in your life. We need to seek direction from God and everything that we do will take off. Some pastors are afraid that their Churches are not going to grow. Take heart and do the work of the Lord for at the right time God will bring the increase. Is. 48: 17-18 "Thus saith the Lord, Thy Redeemer, the Holy One of Israel; I am the Lord thy God which teacheth thee to profit, which leadeth thee by the way that thou shouldest go. O that thou hadst hearkened to my commandments! Then had thy peace been as a river, and thy righteousness as the waves of the sea." God is prepared to lead us and show us what to do so that we will be prosperous in this world, but the sad thing is we do not listen to God when he is speaking to us. Many Christians have not even learned how to hear form God. If you want to know more about hearing from God then get my book entitled "Effective Prayers". God is able to lead every child of His to be successful and prosperous in this world. If we want to succeed in this world then we have to listen to what God wants us to do. We need to listen to God and we will be successful and we will not be afraid that what we are doing is going to fail.

- **Fear of growing old:** Many people are afraid of growing old. There are so many products out there for people to use to cover their wrinkle faces and necks. There a lot of procedure out there for people to do to look young. But let me tell you no matter what you do you cannot stop growing old. We spend money to go under the knife and use botox in our wrinkle faces and other places in order to look young. So far as the Word of God says we are going to grow old, we can stop our wrinkle faces for a short period of time but it will never stop us from growing old. Looking at Is. 46: 3-4 "Hearken unto me, O house of Jacob, and all the remnant of the house of Israel, which are borne by me from the belly, which are carried from the womb: And even to your old age I am he; and even to hoar hairs will I carry you." God has promised to see us through even in our old age, then why should we be afraid of growing old. The Lord God has promised and he will never fail us. Our Heavenly Father will see us through this life and if we keep the faith to the end, then we will meet face to face with God the Father, God the Son, and God the Holy Spirit. Do not be afraid of growing old.

- **Fear of man:** Looking at Prov. 29:25 "The fear of man bringeth a snare: but whoso putteh his trust in the Lord shall be safe. A snare is a trap that is used to capture an animal or something. If you are afraid of a person then it is like setting a trap for yourself. You will be shaken whenever that person speaks. That person will be like a demigod to you. We need to show respect to our bosses at work but we should not be afraid of them. Many people are afraid of others due to fear and intimidation. In our schools we get many kids being bully by others to make their schooling experience a nightmare. My little girl Jedidah was being bully in school. I went to the school several times but nothing could stop these bullies. Without my knowledge, Abigail, the older sister went to the school and one after another told those bullying her little sister to stop or she would come to the school to beat anyone bullying her sister. I was not happy when I heard that Abigail had been to the school, but thank God the bully stop. Even in the Church, there are some people when they speak, it is final and they do not want anyone to challenge or speak their mind. Everyone is afraid of such people and they control the Church. We should not be afraid of anyone, at work, in the home, in the church or in any other place. The fear of a man will enslave you. We have to know that fear is not from God. The spirit of fear is an evil spirit from the camp of the enemy. The Bible says God has given us the spirit of power, love, and sound mind. God has given us the power to live as Children of God and to destroy the works of the enemy. If we do not know the works of the enemy then how can we destroy them? I will do my best for us to know most of the works of the enemy so that we will be able to destroy any work that he enemy may bring in our lives in the church, home or work places. God has given us power so that we will be able to evangelize the world. We need to bring people to Christ and we need the power to do that. Power is defined by Merriam Webster as the ability to act or produce an effect. Power is simply the ability to do work. Therefore God has given us power to work in the Kingdom of God.

2. **Accusation:** This means to bring an unfounded allegation against someone. One major work of the devil is to bring an allegation against Christians before God. This means the devil accuses Christians before God. The devil also accuses God to Christians. The devil also accuses you to yourself. Looking at Rev. 12: 10 "And I heard a loud voice saying in heaven, Now is come salvation, and strength, and the kingdom of our God, and the power of his Christ: for the accuser of our brethren is cast down, which accused them before our God day and night." The devil accuses the Christians day and night before God.

   a. **Accusing God to the Christians:** The devil will tell the Christian if God is a God answering prayer why is it that your prayer has not been answered? Do you think your God is caring and all-knowing, then why so many evil things in this world? Satan will do his best to accuse God for the evil things that he will do on this earth. The battle ground is our mind. The enemy will come with all sort of nasty things just to waiver our faith in God. 2 Cor. 10: 3 -5 "For though we walk in the flesh, we do not war after the flesh: (For the weapons of our warfare are not carnal, but mighty through God to the pulling down of strong holds;) Casting down imaginations, and every high thing that exalteth itself against the knowledge of God, and bringing into captivity every though to the obedience of Christ." St. Paul is telling us that we do not war after the flesh. Which means too much talking and thinking are not going to get us out of a problem. It is a spiritual warfare which can only be fought through effective prayers. If you want to know how to pray effectively then get a copy of my first book entitle "Effective Prayers" at wwwAmazon.com. Maybe you are lady who has been praying for a partner for quite a long time without seeing any result. The enemy is wearying you down and you are about to give up. This is the time that God is going to show up. I will tell you to hold on for your breakthrough. The weapons of our warfare; which means we have so many and different kinds of weapons which God has given us to fight Satan and his forces. We will get to know these weapons as we read the Bible in search for them. Let me give you an example; for instant, you are praying and you do not see any result, then the enemy will tell you that your God is a weak God who cannot answer your prayers. Your weapon for this thought is in Ps. 65: 2 "O thou that hearest prayer, unto thee shall all flesh come." My God is a prayer answering God, so no matter what He will answer my prayer. Even if He does not answer me, I will continue to worship Him. You hit the devil with a nail on the forehead and he will stop worrying you. St. Paul is telling us to cast down imaginations (not only once, for the devil will come in with so many imaginations.) Where do we imagine things? Our mind; that is why I said the battle ground is our mind. So anytime a thought comes into your mind; that is not in line with the Word of God, just cast out. You have to do it yourself for nobody can do it for you. St. Paul continues to say that, anything that exalts itself against the knowledge of God, that the devil, will bring into your mind, cast it out. How can we bring our thoughts to the obedience of Christ? It is by reading and meditating on the Word of God and being prepared to put the Word into practice.

b. **Accusing Christians to God:** One of the main works of the enemy is to accuse Christians before God. The devil is so crafty but he is always a failure. Let us look at Job 1: 6-12 "Now there was a day when the sons of God came to present themselves before the Lord, and Satan came also among them. And the Lord said unto Satan, Whence comest thou? Then Satan answered the Lord, and said, from going to and fro in the earth, and from walking up and down in it. And the Lord said unto Satan, Hast thou considered my servant Job, that there is none like him in the earth, a perfect and upright man, one that feareth God, and escheweth evil? Then Satan answered the Lord, and said, Doth Job fear God for nought? Hast not thou made an hedge about all that he hath on every side? Thou hast blessed the work of his hands, and his substance is increased in the land. But put forth thine hand now, and touch all that he hath, and he will curse thee to the face. And the Lord said unto Satan, Behold, all that he hath is in thy power; only upon himself put not forth thine hand. So Satan went forth from the presence of the Lord." Satan is a busy bee. When God asked Satan "where are you coming from?" Satan replies he has been walking up and down through the earth. Wherever the devil goes, there is trouble, for he is a trouble maker. He went before the presence of God just to accuse Job. He is an accuser and he accuses every Christian to God, but the Blood that speaks better things is there to speak for us. God is really protecting His people and Satan is aware of such protection. Satan said God has made a hedge around Job, and that was the reason why Job was worshiping Him. Satan was wrong, for Job was worshiping God for he has chosen from his own free will to worship his God who was his creator. Job loved the Lord. As soon as you choose to worship God then God makes a covenant with you. In the New Testament this covenant is sealed with the blood of Jesus Christ. In this covenant all God's promises in His Word belongs to you. You are the apple of God's eye and He protects you and your whole family daily from the schemes of Satan. Satan tried so many times to worked evil against Job but he could not because of the protection of God. Therefore, Satan thought Job was worshiping God because of God's protection. God knew the heart of Job so He said "Satan I have given you the mandate go, and everything that Job has is now in your power do whatever you want but do not touch Job. Satan destroyed everything that Job had yet Job worshiped God. This is my personal stand nothing will happen to me on this earth for me to stop worshiping My God and Savior Jesus Christ. Satan will use every means to weaver your faith in God, but stand still for you shall see the salvation of our God.

c. **Accusing Christians to Christians:** There is a lot of accusations and back-biting going on in the Church. Members of a congregation may be talking a lot about their pastor and his wife for no apparent reason. The pastor has his/her favorites in the church, especially the well to do people. The pastor visits some people's house but he/she has never been to my house. The pastor is misusing the church funds, which, may not be true. When such a thing happens then you know the enemy is at work; the devil just wants to tarnish the good work of the pastor. There are people who will never do anything to help in the church, but when someone is tirelessly working hard on any project in the church, some people will do their best to sabotage the good things that are going on. A church may have a building fund, scholarship fund, Pastor's appreciation day and many others. Some of the members will start talking about how the church is taking too much money from them. Usually those talking are the people who do not give to the church. You may not be rich but the little that you can give for God's work is well pleasing and welcome. If there is a sex scandal in the Church, then there is going to be a lot of accusation and if nothing is done by the leaders of the church to nib the accusations in the bud, its ripple effect may cause damages to the Church. One person may start accusing another person in the church just because of jealousy and this may become like a ripple effect and unfounded allegation may start eating up the church. Satan is so crafty that he may bring in accusations, lies, rumors bickering and backbiting to destroy a church. Some of the members will leave to other churches. We should be very careful what we say about others. Can you substantiate what you are saying? If the person you are talking about is around will you be able to say what you are saying? If not then stop talking about others for it will not profit you.

d. **Accusing a person to self (That is accusing you to yourself):** The devil will accuse you to yourself. Identity crisis is one of the major things that the enemy uses in accusing Christians and unbelievers to themselves. One may see himself or herself as a good for nothing or unworthy person and in so doing belittling himself or herself. The enemy will say there is nothing good that may come out of you or from your house and if you believe it, then you have given the enemy the chance to get at you. Let us say, for instance you are a short man, then the devil will say you will not get any beautiful lady to marry, because you are too short. If you give in to what the devil is saying then you will never get a partner. The devil will also tell a beautiful lady, you are too fat and because you are not skinny you are not beautiful and no man will ever ask your hand in marriage. The beautiful lady will give into what the devil is telling her and she may start to see herself ugly. The devil will bring competition between the ladies in the church who will be talking about nothing but who dress well for church. The devil also comes in with comparison telling a talented person someone is more talented than him/her. Satan knows what he is doing so do not be little him. Satan and his forces will do their best to hinder the prayers of the saints and he will turn around to tell you, you do not know how to pray or you are not important to God, that is why, your prayers are not answered. The enemy knows what he is doing, to tarnish the Christians faith in God. Christians can only destroy the works of the devil through the power of the Holy Ghost. Satan will always use your past life to accuse you. When you sin against God then Satan comes in with accusation that you do not fit to be a child of God. Please do not allow the enemy to use your past to discredit you. I met a woman who practiced prostitution in

Germany. When she became a Christian, she was worried about her past life. She kept her past life a secret from the husband and children but she was afraid that a time would come when her children would know about her terrible past life. She was a confused and perplexed person. She was afraid of her past life. I read from the Word of God and the Word set her free from her past and fears. Let us look at Hebrew 9: 14 "How much more shall the blood of Christ, who through the eternal Spirit offered himself without spot to God, purge your conscience from dead works to serve the living God?" I let this woman know that the blood of Jesus Christ has purged or cleaned our conscience from dead works (past sins) so that we will have a good and clean conscience to serve God. The devil can worry about my past life but I do not have time to think about my past. Looking at Phil. 3:14 "I Press toward the mark for the prize of the high calling of God in Christ Jesus." This is what we have to do instead of filling our minds with unwanted thoughts from the camp of the devil. I met another man who had sex with his own sister, and later became a Christian and thought that sin would never be forgiven him. I had to get him through a lot of Scriptures for him to be set free from the enemy. Always think about the things of God, read your Bible daily and pray rather than allowing the enemy to use you to accuse yourself. If you have nothing to do then the enemy may come in to give you something to do. Use your time wisely and get closer to God every minute. Another thing is self-image. As Christians we have our image in Christ. You do not need to be like someone (dress like someone, shape your hair like someone or see yourself as such a person) before you can feel good about yourself. Dress nicely and modest, and enjoy life in Christ Jesus

Chapter Four

Divorce

<u>The works of Satan and the evil spirits</u>

The devil is so cunning and crafty that we need not to underestimate his power and wisdom. "Lucifer, the bearer of light become the prince of darkness, has earned his name of Satan, "the adversary". He is the enemy of God, of man, of all that is good. It is no part of wisdom to underestimate an enemy. It is stupidity to cultivate an ignorance of the enemy to the point of blindness to his existence; for in such blindness it is impossible to face an enemy, let alone hold him at bay or conquer him. This is to invite defeat, to welcome slavery, to yield supinely to a conquest that in this case is radical, irrevocable, eternal."[10] It is with stupidity to declare non- existence of the devil. One of Satan's major works is deception so he may deceive you to believe in the nonexistence of Satan. He will fool many even highly educated people to believe that there is no God. Looking at Ps. 14:1 "The fool hath said in his heart, There is no God. They are corrupt, they have done abominable works, there is none that doeth good." The Bible says "you are foolish to say that there is no God. The devil can corrupt your mind and your heart if you give him the chance. If one believes that there is no God, then, there is high possibility for such a person, also to believe in the non-existence of the devil. Such a person may believe in him/ herself. Everything revolves around self. He/she can do all things through his/her own strength. Where do you get your strength? It is God who gives you the strength. Ps 29:6 "The Lord will give strength unto his people; the Lord will bless his people with peace." So it is God who gives us strength and also blesses us with His peace. One has to think positively about what he/she can do. Positive thinking is good but it should be in line with the Word of God. If what you are thinking is ungodly, then it is not positive thinking but devilish. The devil is doing its best even to corrupt the church into thinking that it is all right to divorce, but the Word of God says otherwise.

Divorce: Divorce is from the camp of the enemy. Satan is really happy to see couples divorcing their marriages. Divorce rate in the church is now high that even it is easy to see ministers (Pastors) in their second and third marriages. Let all pastors divorce their wives, it does not change the Word of God. Looking at Malachi 2:14-16 "Yet ye say, Wherefore? Because the Lord hath been <u>witness</u> between thee and the wife of thy youth, against whom thou hast dealt treacherously: yet is she thy <u>companion,</u> and the wife of thy <u>covenant</u>. And did not he make one? Yet had he the residue of the spirit. And wherefore one? That he might seek a godly seed. Therefore take heed to your spirit, and let none deal treacherously against the wife of his youth. For the Lord, the God of Israel, saith that he <u>hateth</u> putting away (divorce). For one covereth <u>violence</u> with his garment, saith the Lord of hosts: therefore take heed to your spirit, that ye deal not <u>treacherously</u>. Every Christian believes in the Old and New Testaments. This is because the Christian believes that the Creator God of the Old Testament is the same Redeemer God of the New Testament..." I do not know whether some ministers have this verses in their Bible. God says he hates divorce. This is the first time that I have seen the word hate use by God. He did not say I dislike divorce, but I HATE. The word hate has a connotation attach to it. Do not do it or you deal treacherously, which means you are treading on dangerous grounds. It is deceitful and dangerous to divorce. It is not easy to accept this but that is the truth. Satan has made divorce to look so glamorous and exiting that even Pastors are divorcing. Let every pastor on this earth divorce, it does not change the word of God. Let us look at something important, for Malachi Chapter 2 talks about divorce and Malachi Chapter 3 talks about tithes and offering. I am yet to hear messages on Malachi Chapter 2. Many pastors will go pass Malachi Chapter 2 and talk only about Malachi 3, because Malachi 3 will bring money into the church but for Malachi Chapter 2, those who had divorce would not be comfortable, and may leave the church. The pastors now preach what the members want to hear and not what God wants them to bring to the congregation. God hates divorce. God is telling us that He has been a witness in every Christian marriage. What does it mean to be a witness? Merriam Webster Dictionary defines, witness as one asked to be present at a transaction so as to be able to testify to its having taken place. In every Christian marriage, we pray and ask for the presence of the Lord. God is telling us that He was present at your marriage so He is able to testify that your marriage did take place. Do you want to disannul something, which God has been a witness? Marriage is so special that God put His signature on your wedding or marriage certificate. It is important to talk to and hear from God before you get into marriage. Every marriage has its own peculiar problems but if the two people involved are prepared to work together and establish the marriage on the Word of God then the marriage will be on a solid foundation. The Word of God says your wife is your companion. What is a companion? Companion is a helpful friend, one who is a buddy, one you can share your secrets. If you start hiding certain things from your wife, then you do not see her as your companion. When the link of companionship is destroyed then the marriage is on its way to divorce. You make a marriage covenant with your wife, when your get married. What is a covenant? According to Merriam Webster Dictionary, a covenant is a written agreement or promise usually under seal between two or more parties especially for the performance of some action. Therefore, a Christian marriage is an agreement between the two parties to be bound by the holy matrimony and to live together as husband and wife till death do depart. In the Old Testament a covenant was sealed with the blood of sheep or goat but, the New Testament covenant is sealed with the Blood of Jesus. Therefore, we the New Testament Christians sealed our marriages with the Blood of Jesus Christ. If your marriage is sealed with the Blood of Jesus then God will hate to see divorce. God did not say "I dislike divorce" for that will have made it okay to divorce but He said "I hate divorce." Breaking a covenant is detrimental to a Christian well being. The Word of God continues to say divorce breads violence and you are treading on a dangerous ground when you divorce. Why should we as Christians be so interested in something that God hates? The only person who loves divorce is Satan so he will do his best to steal the happiness in marriage, and kill and destroy any marriage. Christians are saying, we love what Satan love. The we are not walking worthy of the vocation of our calling. Looking at Rom. 1:28-32 "And even as they did not like to retain God in their knowledge, God gave them over to a reprobate mind, to do those things which were not convenient; Being filled with all unrighteousness, fornication, wickedness, covetousness, maliciousness, full of envy, murderer, debate, deceit, malignity, whisperers, Backbiters, haters of God, despiteful, proud, boasters, inventors of evil things, disobedient to parents, Without understanding, covenant-breakers, without natural affection, implacable, unmerciful: Who knowing the judgment of God, that they which commit such things are worthy of death, not only do the same, but have pleasure in them that do them." There is a lot of the works of the devil mention in these verses but I am only concerned about covenant-breakers, and I will do my best to treat the rest later on. Breaking a covenant is a sin in the sight of God. Covenant breaking is among the things which if one commits he/she is worthy of death. As soon as you married, you enter into a marriage covenant with your partner, so your wife is your covenant wife. When you divorce, you have broken the covenant which is a sin before God and the judgment of God is that you are worthy of death so, this is one reason why God hates divorce. Most children from divorce marriages if not properly taken care of will end up becoming violent kids, which may affect their future behavior, attitudes, and life. If the kids do not give their lives to Jesus and forgive the parents and themselves, some of them may think they were the cause of the marriage melt down between their parents. They may live in fear that their marriages are also not going to work. Some of the kids may think of not marrying at all. Note as parents what, decision you take today affect the whole family, now and the future.

I believe with all my heart that divorce is never an option in marriage dispute. In Matt19: 3-10 "The Pharisees also came unto him, tempting him, and saying unto him, Is it lawful for a man to put away his wife for every cause? And he answered and said unto them, Have ye not read, that he which made them at the beginning made them male and female. And said, For this cause shall a man leave father and mother, and shall cleave to his wife: and the twain shall be one flesh? Wherefore they are no more twain, but one flesh. What therefore God hath joined together, let no man put asunder. They say unto him, Why did Moses then command to give a writing of divorcement, and to put her away? He said unto them, Moses because of the hardness of your hearts suffered you to put away your wives: but from the beginning it was not so. And I say unto you, Whosoever shall put away his wife, except it be for fornication, and shall marry another, committeth adultery: and whoso marrieth her which is put away doth commit adultery. His disciples say unto him, if the case of a man be so with his wife, it is not good to marry." Jesus spelled out for us saying what God has put together (meaning God brings marriages together, witness the marriage and put His signature on your marriage certificate) let no man put asunder. Why do you think the disciples said, then it is not good to marry? It is because they know that there may be a time when the couple may not understand one another and may ask for divorce. If they divorce and remarry then, four people have committed adultery. Looking at 1 Corinth. 6:9-10 "Know ye not that the unrighteous will not inherit the kingdom of God? Be not deceived: neither fornicators, nor idolaters, nor adulterers, nor effeminate, nor abusers of themselves with mankind, nor thieves, nor covetous, nor drunkards, nor revilers, nor extortioners, shall inherit the kingdom of God." If you do not want to enter the kingdom of God, then you can divorce and remarry. If you want to enter the kingdom of God then, if you divorce, you do not marry again. If you want to marry then go back to your wife. In Romans, marriage was used as an illustration of Christ relation to the Church, and it spells out what Jesus said in Matthew. Looking at Rom. 7: 2-3 "For the woman which hath an husband is bound by the law to her husband so long as he liveth; but if the husband be dead, she is loosed from the law of her husband. So then if, while her husband liveth, she be married to another man, she shall be called an adulteress: but if her husband be dead, she is free from that law; so that she is no adulteress, though she be married to another man." One may say this was under the law, and the present day Christian is no more under the law. But let me tell you this is the same law that Jesus also confirmed in Matthew, which means God is not taking light of marriage that is why He hates divorce. I believe the enemy is using divorce as a major weapon against the Church. I personally know some Bishops who are in their second marriage and some pastors who are in their third marriage. Divorce has become the norm of the day but I believe nothing can neutralize the Word of God. Jesus says, if you divorce and remarry you have committed adultery. Why should the disciples say then it is not good to get married? It is because if one commits adultery, then he/she may not inherit the Kingdom of God. Looking at 1 Cor. 6: 9-10 "Know ye not that the unrighteous shall not inherit the kingdom of God? Be not deceived: neither fornicators, nor idolaters, nor adulterers, nor effeminate, nor abusers of themselves with mankind (homosexuals), nor thieves, nor covetous, nor drunkards, shall inherit the kingdom of God." If you commit adultery, you are not going to see the kingdom of God, which means you may miss mark of entering into heaven. This is difficult to believe but that is what the Word of God says. Many pastors and the elders of the church, have divorced and remarried so you will never hear the Word of God about divorce being preach in the church. The Word of God teaches us how we will be able to overcome most of the problems we encounter in our marriages. Looking at the Song of Solomon 2: 15-16 "Takes us the foxes, the little foxes, that spoil the vines: for our vines have tender grapes. My beloved is mine, and I am his: he feedeth among the lilies." The Israelites were farmers so they could understand these verses clearly. Solomon is telling us to take the little foxes that spoil the vine. Looking at the next verse one will know that Solomon was talking about marriage. When a vine is planted then the farmer has to look for means to get rid of the little foxes or they will come in to spoil the vine. The vine is the marriage, and what are the little foxes in marriage? It can be misunderstanding, fighting between the couple, weak finances, abusing one another, and many others. First, each of the couple has to examine him/herself, and know why he /she got into married? If you do not know why you are doing something then it is a disaster in itself. If you do not know why you go to church then you are not yet a Christian. If you know that marriage was ordained by God and as such is sacred then you will enter into marriage with respect to God and your partner. God want us to marry so that we will be able to not only produce, but bring up godly seed. Do you get married because the person was beautiful or financially sound? Then what are you going to do when the beauty start to fade away or if the person becomes financially weak? In marriage, inner qualities are more important than the outward qualities. We have to check our attitudes or characters that we brought into the marriage. If you have a bad attitude, you can stop it and change over. It is a little fox, that can be tamed. If you have a hot anger then you need to go for anger management. Do not take the Word of God lightly and be prepared to walk with God. Looking at Genesis 5: 24 "And Enoch walked with God: and he was not; for God took him." What does it mean to walk with God? It is being prepared to obey the Word of God. For example, God hates divorce and because of that no matter what I will work it out and not get divorce. Then you are walking with God. I will not enter into extramarital affair because the Word of God is against it. Then you are walking with God. We have to study and know the Word of God and to live in line with the Word of God in order to walk with God. We abide by the Word of God then God is going to bless our marriage and our home. Looking at Deuteronomy 30:19-20 "I call heaven and earth to record this day against you, that I have set before you life and death, blessing and cursing: therefore choose life, that both thou and thy seed may live: That thou mayest love the Lord thy God, and that thou mayest obey his voice, and that thou mayest cleave unto him: for he is thy life, and the length of thy days." God has set a choice before us. We can either choose life and blessings or death and cursing. God has given us a free will but whatever we choose comes with it consequence. It is a choice to walk with God. If you want to walk with God then, you have to love God. If you love God then you will not like to do something that will be detrimental to your relationship with God. Next, you have to obey God. Which means what God says is what you are prepared to do, even if it go against what you want to do. Lastly you have to cleave unto God. This means you are fussed into God and there is no difference between you and God. You live by God's Word. The Word is firmly, established in the heavens. Do you know that many Christians are going to be left behind during the Rapture. It is sad, because, many Pastors do not preach about the end times but they preach only what the members want to hear. Preaching now is only on prosperity, blessings, having financial breakthrough, wellbeing, love of God, but nothing on sin, walking worthy of the vocation of your calling, the wrath of God, end-times, and the Rapture. Let me talk a little about the Rapture. The word Rapture cannot be found in the Bible but it is a concept, which, is truly going to proceed, the Second Coming of our Lord and Savoir Jesus Christ. Looking at 1 Thess. 4: 15-18 "For this we say unto you by the word of the Lord, that we which are alive and remain unto the coming of the Lord shall not prevent them which are asleep. For the Lord himself shall descend from heaven with a shout, with the voice of the archangel, and with the trump of God: the dead in Christ shall rise first: Then we which are alive and remain shall be caught up together with them in the clouds, to meet the Lord in the air: and so shall we ever be with the Lord. Wherefore comfort one another with these words." I do not want to get into detail on the topic of the Rapture. During the Rapture, those who are dead in Christ are going to be resurrected with heavenly bodies and those who are still alive are also going to get heavenly bodies and are going to be caught up together with those who are resurrected in Christ in the air to meet the Lord Jesus. This is what the Bible scholars have given it the term Rapture. The sad thing is that it is not all Christians who are going to be Rapture, but those who live their lives according to the Word of God. You may not like this message but if you divorce then you are not living your live according to the Word of God. May be the enemy is using divorce as a ploy to get many Christians to be left behind. I do not know but that may be Satan's major ploy. If you want to know more about the Rapture then look for the movie entitled "Left Behind part 1 and 2 and watch them. Divorce is not an option so let's get to the Word of God to mend our broken marriage relationships. So far as we are in this shattered world our marriages are going to face problems. How we react to the problems and difficulties will determine the cause of our marriages. Every marriage faces problems, so you are not alone, just rely on the Word of God to solve any challenges that you will face in your marriage life. Let me tell you, you do not see God's signature with your natural eyes but with the spiritual eyes, you will be able to see His signature on your marriage certificate. God has endorsed your marriage, so He does not want you to put it asunder or divorce. There are so many things that the devil can use to cause divorce in marriage. Let me mention a few: a) The husband becomes bossy and treats the wife as if she is a servant or a trash. b) Weak finance or poor financial management may also wreck a marriage. The devil will put you in poverty in such a way as to make your marriage life miserable. The wife may be doing well than the husband so she may like to keep a separate bank account, but when the two are able to keep one account and are faithful with the way the money is spent, the finances of the family will be well kept. c) The woman may be abusing the husband or the vice versa. Abuse includes words of insults, moral abuse, physical abuse, throwing punches at each other, spiritual abuse, not praying with one another. d) Ungodly counseling from friends and close relatives. Mothers-in law who control marriages of their son or daughter telling them what to do. e) Weak communication between couples, can wreck the marriage. A wife may talk or text on the phone for hours with friends but will not call the husband to talk to him. Let the husband calls and she has no time for the husband. You need to sit down and talk or you will destroy your marriage. f) Sexual affair outside your marriage will break your marriage. God only recognizes marriage couple having sex. It is an abomination to have sex outside your marriage. Heb. 13:4 "Marriage is honourable in all, and the bed undefiled: but whoremongers and adulterers God will judge." When you divorce and remarried you become an adulterer and God will judge you. I do not know how but that is what His Word. God says it is only sex in marriage, that, He recognizes. The bed is undefiled, which means sex in marriage is clean before God. f) Another thing, that destroys, marriage is when, the husband or wife does not want to have sex. I have known a marriage couple who have not have sex for over three good years because the wife does not want it. Sometimes, it is the man, who does not want to have sex. This is the work of the enemy and we have to pray against such works. Looking at 1 Cor. 7:3-5 "Let the husband render unto the wife due benevolence: and likewise also the wife unto the husband. The wife hath not power of her own body, but the husband: and likewise also the husband hath not power of his own body, but the wife. Defraud ye not one the other, except it be with consent for a time, that ye may give yourselves to fasting and prayer; and come together again, that Satan tempt you not for your incontinency." There we are, for your wife has no control over her body and the vice versa. Sex cannot be taken out of marriage. I will say once a week is okay for me but what about my partner? This has to be discussed between the couple. Sometimes the wife may be tired due to the day's work and the husband has to understand but this should not be everyday you are tired. If the husband is growing old and experiencing erectile dysfunctional then he should be bold to discuss it with the wife and look for medication. Please build your marriage on the Word of God and it would stand the test of time. Looking at Prov. 14:1 "Every wise woman buildeth her house: but the foolish plucketh it down with her hands." I believe a Christian woman will be so wise to build her house and she will never listen to ungodly counseling but be steadfast in the Word of God. If you are a woman and you are using sex as a weapon, then be very careful or if your husband is not sold out to Christ then he may find solace somewhere. If you are a woman and you insult or curse at your husband for no apparent reason, then note you are tearing down you house with your own hands. Prov. 19:14 "House and riches are the inheritance of fathers: and a prudent wife is from the Lord." I believe every father will like to see wealth and riches in his life time so that he can pass it on to his children. To get a prudent wife a man has to do a lot of praying for God to get you one. What is the meaning of prudent? Merriam Webster defined prudent as marked by wisdom or judiciousness, which means someone who exercises sound judgment. May be you get married without praying for a prudent wife, but it is not late to pray for God to do the makeover. Eph. 5: 22-25 "Wives submit yourselves unto your own husbands, as unto the Lord. For the husband is the head of the wife, even as Christ is the head of the church: and he is the savior of the body. Therefore as the church is subject unto Christ, so let the wives be to their own husbands in everything. Husbands, love your wives, even as Christ also loved the church, and gave himself for it;" This is the core of marriage, for every marriage where the wife sees the husband as the head of the house and give due respect to the husband in every area of life, the marriage will stand. The husband being the head does not make him a boss who mistreats the wife, but he has to love the wife as Jesus did for the church and gave himself for it. In the same way, a husband should love the wife and be prepared even to die for her. If a husband has such a mind he will never mistreat the wife or get himself involve in extra-marital affairs. There will always be peace in the house and your children are going to prosper and see the goodness of the Lord. Another thing that can cause divorce is ungodly counseling. The wife should not listen to friends who are not able to give godly and sound advice. Likewise, the husband should not align himself with good for nothing people who do not live by wise counseling. Looking at Prov. 24: 3-6 "Through wisdom is an house builded; and by understanding it is established: And by knowledge shall the chambers be filled with all precious and pleasant riches. A wise man is strong; yea, a man of knowledge increaseth strength. For by wise counsel thou shalt make thy war: and in the multitude of counselors there is safety." For a marriage couple to build their house they need the wisdom of God. There are two different kind of wisdom; which are the earthly wisdom and the heavenly wisdom, therefore a marriage couple need the heavenly wisdom to keep their marriage going. Looking at James 3: 13-18 "Who is a wise man and endued with knowledge among you? Let him shew out of a good conversation his works with meekness of wisdom. But if ye have bitter envying and strife in your hearts, glory not, and lie not against the truth. This wisdom descendeth not from above, but is earthly, sensual, devilish. For where envying and strife is, there is confusion and every evil work. But the wisdom that is from above is first pure, then peaceable, gentle, and easy to be entreated, full of mercy and good fruits, without partiality, and without hypocrisy. And the fruit of righteousness is sown in peace of them that make peace." What is wisdom? The Merriam Webster defines wisdom as a wise attitude, belief, or cause of action. This means a wise person who is able to make a sound judgment. We can see that with the earthly wisdom, one always want to show that she/he is smarter than others and this breed strife and envy. There is cheating and confusion with the earthly wisdom, therefore a couple who build their house with earthly wisdom will tear the house apart, ending in divorce. Why? Because the earthly wisdom is sensual and devilish, that is it comes from the camp of Satan. With the earthly wisdom, you always think about yourself, and do not care about your partner or anybody. You always want to be powerful and do not want anybody to challenge you. You always want to be in the front seat. So far, as you are comfortable you are okay, and do not care what, someone is felling, or going through. You always want to have your own way through any means fair or foul. The wisdom that is from above or the heavenly wisdom is first of all pure, this means any person who lives by this wisdom is pure or does things that are clean or right. She/he has self confidence and do not look down on other people. She /he has the respect for other people especially, his/her partner and the elderly people. This person recognizes the sanctity of marriage and will never cheat on his/her partner. His or her actions are pure, so whatever she/he says comes out of purity, therefore there is no abuse, or trash talk or curses coming out of the mouth. Looking at Matth 5:8 "Blessed are the pure in heart: for they shall see God." If you want to see God, then you have to be pure in heart, which means you have a soft heart fill with the wisdom of God or God's Word. Then you marriage will be established on a solid foundation, and not on the riches, or things of the world. Secondly, the wisdom that is from above is peaceable, which means any actions that come from the person exercising this wisdom bears the fruit of peace. He/she always seeks peace and is also, a peacemaker. If there is a rift between two people a peacemaker always reconciles those people together. She/he is a peace maker, and do her/his best, to live at peace with all people, including her/his partner. If you call yourself a Christian and is not prepared to make peace then you have to check your way of life or I will say you are not a real Christian. Jesus Christ died in order to bring peace between us (human) and God (the Creator). Christians have also been given, the ministry of reconciliation (that is making peace). Therefore, every child of God should be prepared to make peace with his/her partner when there is a problem or conflict. Looking at Matth. 5:9 "Blessed are the peacemakers: for they shall be called the children of God." If you want to be called a child of God then be prepared to solve the conflict or the problem between you and your partner. The heavenly wisdom is also gentle. Any course of action taken by a person who is exercising this wisdom is gentle. The husband is gentle with the wife, and speaks gently to her. The wife also exercises restrain and respects the husband. In daily decision making there is a team work with compromise and no ill feelings. One does not say I stand by my decision and unless you agree with me there is no compromise. Looking at Amos 3:3 Can two walk together, except they be agreed?" Therefore marriage couple can stay together if they agree on the major and minor life issues. There will be agreement if they apply the heavenly wisdom in the marriage. The heavenly wisdom is also easy to be entreated, which means it is not difficult to talk to such a person as he/she is prepared to talk and to say "I am sorry" if the person is at fault. Some people are really, difficult to be entreated as they stand by what they say and are not prepared to give in. It makes it difficult to talk to such a person when there is a problem in the marriage. If the party involve in a marriage are both easy to be entreated then divorce will not be an option, for it is taken off the table. In this world there will be problems everywhere, including, marriages, but if the party involve are prepared to respect the Word of God and abide by the Word, then the marriage will survive the test of time. The heavenly wisdom is full of mercy, which means such a person is full of compassion so he/she forgives so easily without any strings attach. The husband always do his best to understand the wife and the vice versa. The heavenly wisdom is also without partiality and hypocrisy, which means a person exercising the heavenly wisdom, is able to make a sound judgment without partiality or favoritism. Such a person is not a hypocrite. The Merriam Webster defines hypocrite as a person who acts in contradiction to his or her stated beliefs or feelings. Therefore, any person exercising the heavenly wisdom will not act contrary to the Word of God. It is through the heavenly wisdom that a house is builed. Where can we get the wisdom of God? Looking at Jam. 1:5 "If any of you lack wisdom, let him ask of God, that giveth to all men liberally, and upbraideth not; and it shall be given him." Ask for the wisdom of God and it shall be given unto you. It is my prayer that the wisdom of God will be our portion as beloved Children of God, so that our marriages will be builed on the wisdom of God. A man with the wisdom of God will never beat the wife or make the wife a punching bag. Such a man will not abuse the wife in any other way. The woman with the wisdom of God will make sure her house is in good shape. Looking at Prov. 14:1 "Every wise woman buildeth her house: but foolish plucketh it down with her hands." I believe Christian women will be wise enough to build their houses, that is, to see to the wellbeing of their marriage. The next thing that established a house is understanding. What is understanding? The Merriam Webster defines understanding as a mental grasp, comprehension. It is the ability to comprehend and be thoughtful and considerate. Looking at Prov. 2: 1-2 "My son, if thou wilt receive my words, and hide my commandments with thee; So that thine incline thou ear unto wisdom, and apply thine heart to understanding." The Word of God is showing us how we will be able to get the wisdom and understanding that come from God. First, we have to receive the Word of God and hide the Word within us. This means we are prepared to know the Word of God and to live by the Word. There should be a daily application of the Word in our lives. Listen, the Word of God, shows that we understand with our heart and not our mind. The thought process is done in the mind but it has to be sunk into the heart for you to understand what is going on. The husband has to put himself in the shoes of the wife and the verse versa. When this is done each one will be careful what he/she will say or do to the other. Looking at Prov. 16: 22 "Understanding is a wellspring of life unto him that hath it: but the instruction of fools is folly." Understanding is the wellspring of life for your marriage, so your marriage life will be till death do depart us, if the couple are endow with the understanding that come from the throne of God. Do not lean on your personal or human understanding but the understanding that comes from the throne of God. Prov. 3: 5-7 "Trust in the Lord with all thine heart; and lean not unto thine own understanding. In all thy ways acknowledge him, and he shall direct thy paths. Be not wise in thy own eyes: fear the Lord, and depart from evil." When we trust in the Lord, he will direct our path. God will direct us to greener pastures and we will see the goodness of God. The fear of God will help us to depart from all evil ways including lies, theft and sexual immoralities. And this will let our marriages become strong. The understanding that come from the throne of God is needed for every marriage to survive. Our personal understanding is shallow and hollow and will not stand the test of time. We need the wisdom and the understanding that comes from God for our marriages to stand the wiles and schemes of Satan and his forces who are seeking every marriage to break as divorce is from his camp.

Knowledge is the next component needed in every marriage. The knowledge of the Word of God about our marriages will be important for us to hold and keep our marriages as precious and dear to our hearts. What is knowledge? Merriam Webster defines knowledge as the sum of what is known: the body of truth, information and principles acquire by humankind. The knowledge that marriage is sacred is very important to us as Christians. This means marriage is something, which, has been set apart for the worship of our God. It is holy in the eyes of God. Gen. 2: 24 "Therefore shall a man leave his father and mother, and shall cleave unto his wife: and they shall be one flesh. And they were both naked, the man and his wife, and were not ashamed." We have to know that God want us to move from our parents home set up our own so that the marriage will not be controlled by either of the parents. I will advice the in-laws to work on their own marriages instead of the marriages of their kids. Marriage is between the husband and the wife, and it should not be controlled by any other person, including family members and friends. If we want our marriage to be filled with precious and pleasant riches then the knowledge of God about the married is very important. The married couple can be naked in front of one another but they will not be ashamed. This is a good knowledge, for if one starts to feel embarrassed when naked in front of the partner then something is wrong. Husbands have to know what God expect of them as husbands and their duties according to the Word of God and likewise, the wives. Looking at, 1 Tim 5: 8 "But if any provide not for his own, and specially for those of his own house, he hath denied the faith, and is worse than an infidel." Therefore as Christian parents, we cannot neglect our children, we need to work hard to take care of our kids. As parents we need to create a peaceful home for our children to be at peace and safe, when they are in the house. We do not have to do things like smoking in the presence of the kids, for they are also going to learn how to smoke. Note that the Surgeon Doctor says "Smoking is detrimental to your health," then why do you smoke? Knowledge is power but knowledge of the Word of God concerning your marriage is supernaturally powerful. Any marriage that lacks the knowledge of God will not stand the test of time and may eventually be destroyed. Hosea 4: 6 "My people are destroyed for lack of knowledge: because thou hast rejected knowledge, I will also reject thee, that thou shalt be no priest to me: seeing thou hast forgotten the law of thy God, I will also forget thy children." It is God's word that gives us knowledge about our marriage so when we reject the Word of God then we reject knowledge and for lack of knowledge the marriage will end up in divorce. Let me tell you marriage is a war, for Satan wants every marriage to end up in divorce. But, by wise counseling you will make your war, therefore, godly counseling is needed for our marriages to be fruitful. What is godly or wise counseling? This is an advice given base on the Word of God. Godly advice or counseling is most of the time not according to what we expect, for it is not easy to listen and live by the Word of God. Satan always will make it difficult for us to live by wise counseling. Satan will always make an easy way for you so if you do not take care you will choose the easy way out, which may be from the devil. Going for counseling from unbelievers who have PhD in psychology will not solve your marital problems but look for a true pastor who lives according to the Word of God to give you a godly advice and your marriage will stand, for you will be able to fight your life and marriage war through godly counseling. God has given us our own wills so it is up to us to take godly counseling or take our own way, which, may lead to divorce in the marriage. That is why Prov. 3: 5-6 says "Trust in the Lord with all thine heart; and lean not unto thine own understanding. In all thy ways acknowledge him, and he shall direct thy paths." If a couple want God to direct their marriage then they need to trust in the Lord with all their heart, and they should not lean on their own understanding, which may lead them to folly and to hurt one another. It is not easy trusting in the Lord, for we cannot do that with our sight but by faith. Faith only comes by hearing and hearing by the Word of God. Therefore, we need to daily study the Word and live as the Word says. As we put the Word of God into practice, our faith will be strong and we will see the hand of God working miracles in every area of our lives. Couples need to read and pray daily together. Sometimes due to different work schedule it makes it impossible for partners to come together to fellowship in the Lord. Also, when there is an enmity between the couple and they do not talk to each other then it becomes difficult to pray together, so the man may pray on his own and the wife like wise. Communication between the couple is very important and marriage couple should do their best to talk to each other even in time of difficulties and rifts. When you do not communicate then the rift between you widens up. We do not have to shout at one another during the act of communication. We do not need trash talk but rather words that are meaningful to express our feelings. Partners should be prepared to be good listener when your partner is talking and the verse visa. If you are at fault be prepared to say "I am sorry" and ask for forgiveness. The men you do not need to be macho or you will destroy your marriage. The couple should be prepared to read the Bible, pray, and destroy the work of the enemy together in their everyday life. They may be working on a different schedules but this can be done during their time off. I think if you want to do it then the couple will be able to make a time for it. It is good to make money to take care of the family but it is better to pray together, for the family that prays together stays together. Marriage is so important in the eyes of God so we should not take light of marriage. I think God is so much concern about marriage that He used it as figurative in the union of the Church to Himself. After the Rapture, all Christians (Christians who are raised from dead and rapture with Christians who are living and walking in the Word of God and Christians who are able to go through the tribulation) will be the bride for the marriage of the Lamb. Looking at Rev. 19:7-9 "Let us be glad and rejoice, and give honor to him: for the marriage of the Lamb is come, and his wife hath made herself ready". God is so much concerned about marriage between the church and Jesus Christ that, God wants us to experience the heavenly marriage. That is the reason why God institute the matrimonial marriage on earth. Satan is an enemy of God and any person who will ally or be friend with God, so Satan and his wicked spirits will do their best to chaos into every marriage. Therefore, Christians, have to be wise and build their marriages on the Word of God.

Chapter Five

Deception

3. **Deception:** Looking at Rev. 12: 9 "And the great dragon was cast out, that old serpent, called the Devil, and Satan, which deceiveth the whole world; he was cast out into the earth, and his angels were cast out with him." What is deception? Merriam Webster defines deception as something that deceives. This means something is false or one is trick in believing in a false statement or making something that is not true to become true. Satan used deception in his first act in dealing with human for Eve to sin against God. Gen. 3: 1-7 "Now the serpent was more subtil than any beast of the field which the Lord God had made. And he said unto the woman, Yea, hath God said, Ye shall not eat of every tree of the garden? And the woman said unto the serpent, We may eat of the fruit of the trees of the garden: But of the fruit of the tree which is in the midst of the garden, God hath said, Ye shall not eat of it, neither shall ye touch it, least ye die. And the serpent said unto the woman, Ye shall not surely die: For God doth know that in the day ye eat thereof, then your eyes shall be opened, and ye shall be as gods, knowing good and evil. And when the woman saw that the tree was good for food, and that it was pleasant to the eyes, and a tree to be desired to make one wise, she took of the fruit thereof, and did eat, and gave also unto her husband with her; and he did eat." Satan used a combination of deception, lust of the flesh, lust of the eyes, and the pride of life, to get to Adam and Eve. I want you to know his technique has not changed so Satan is going about with deception, lust of the flesh, lust of the eyes and pride of life for us to sin against our God. The pride of life for we want to be famous and popular so that everyone will love us and worship us so that we will be just like a god and Satan is using, power, riches sex and cheap popularity as a way out. Satan was able to get Adam and Eve because they wanted to be as god knowing good and evil. What a deception. They thought the fruit would make them wise, so the enemy caused them to believe a lie. Eve saw that the fruit was good to be eaten. The enemy used her eyes to entice her. The lust of the flesh at work. Satan has not changed his tricks so we as

Christians need to be very careful always reading and putting the Word of God into practice or we may fall for the wiles of the enemy. Let us do everything in Christ Jesus instead of seeking cheap popularity let us seek God and let Him make us what He wants us to be. Satan is so cunning that we as Christians have to be careful and live daily in Christ or the enemy may get us. A couple may be facing difficulties in their marriage and the enemy may tell them the only option is to divorce. First, the Christian couple has to know that the problems they are facing are from the enemy. The couple needs to sit down and weigh their options in line with the Word of God. Communicate with each other and find solution to the problems. Do your best to live according to the Word of God and your marriage will turn around and be fruitful. May be you were called for interview for your dream job but you were not able to get this dream job. Then the devil will come in and tell you, your God does not care about you. If you accept that then the enemy will waiver your faith in God. You may loose a love one (your mother, father, sister, brother, a wife, a husband, a son, a daughter or a dear friend), the enemy may come in and tell lies to you that God does not care. Please do not listen to Satan for our God is a loving and a caring God. Satan deceives the whole world, so he can deceive anyone except you daily abide in Jesus. Your titles are nothing to Satan, so you can be a Bishop, an Apostle, Prophet, Elder, Honorable Reverend so, so and so, Satan is not afraid of you. Satan is only afraid of one who is totally sold out to Jesus. The one who reads the Word of God daily and put the Word into practice. If one of your feet is in the church and other in the world, then Satan is not afraid of you. Let me tell you a story. I was working in a Diamond mines in Ghana, as a Mining Supervisor, so I saw diamonds every blessed day for three good years. I decided that my Jesus was more precious than diamonds so I did not steal. The salary was too small and it was a monthly salary. If I changed my salary into dollars it will be $80.00 per month but I decided I would not steal. It was difficult living on this mean salary but I decided I would not steal. One time my mother asked me, "have you saved some money since you started working?" I said no. "What are you doing with your life", she replied. I said I paid my tithes so I saved my money in the heaven's bank and when I need money I will tell my Heavenly Father and He will give me a foreign currency. She said, "you are not serious in life." When I was about to come to America, I had no money for my air ticket but I cried unto God and I got Dutch guilders from a friend who lives in the Netherlands for the ticket. Let me tell you another story. One of my fellow Mining Supervisor at the mines, once said to me "You are a disgrace to mining engineers, for you have no car, and you wear the same cloth over and over displaying poverty at its best." I did not say anything and moved away for nothing was going to compel me to steal diamonds, for I would not do anything to tarnish the name of Christ Jesus. I left the mines after working there for three solid years. I travelled to Denmark for further studies at the Apostolic Bible College, in Kolding. I returned to Ghana after my studies. I was walking in the streets of Accra and I could hear behind me "Praise the Lord, Praise the Lord." I turned around and it was the Mining Supervisor who told me I was a good for nothing fellow and a disgrace to mining engineers. He has become a Christian and I asked him what happened. The wife who was a pharmacist got pregnant and the Doctors said her child was dead in the womb so she would need a surgery to take the child out. This Supervisor was so depressed and did not know what to do. It then crossed his mind to pray and this was his prayer, "God, I do not know you. Jesus I heard about you but I do not know you, but Robert (me) knows you. If all that Robert was saying about you is true then let my child live and let my wife gave birth sound and save. If you do this for me I and my household will worship you, Jesus." He said he could not eat but just praying the same prayer over and over. He visited the hospital almost everyday to check on the wife. On the third day he visited the Hospital and the Doctors said the child was kicking. He said because I was praying and everyone started laughing at him for they knew him to be unbeliever and the one who tried his best to make life unbearable for Christians. To make a long story short, the wife was able to give birth to a bouncing baby boy. I never preached to this guy but my life spoke to him and he became a Christian. Let us live a life worthy of the vocation of our calling and God will use our life style to bless others. Whatever the enemy will provide is to entice you to sin against your God. I was not married while working in the mines, so my fellow mining supervisors decided to get me a girl friend for they found me to be archaic, outmoded and a queer person without life. I was once in my residence and heard my door bell ringing. I went to the door and opened it. To my surprise was a very tall, slim beautiful lady who entered as soon as I opened the door. I welcomed her and gave her a seat. I gave her something to drink and I went to my room to bring my Bible. To be frank I was shaking but I purposed in my heart that I would not sin against my God. I shared the Bible with her for over one hour till the bus came in to take her to town and she never show up at my door again. What will few hours of pleasure do to me for me to sin against my God? Looking at Prov. 20:17 "Bread of deceit is sweet to a man; but afterwards his mouth shall be filled with gravel." We need to be careful and prayerful or the enemy may come in with the bread of deceit. When we pray, listen to godly advice, and walk according to the Word of God, then we will be able to overcome the enemy.

4. **Temptation:** Another work of the enemy is to bring in temptation. Looking at Mat.4:1 "Then was Jesus led up of the Spirit into wilderness to be tempted of the devil." If the devil even tempted Jesus then he is not afraid to tempt anyone. We need to live daily in Christ or the devil will come in when least expected to tempt us. "It is not a sin to be tempted. Jesus

was tempted, yet he never sinned. Temptation only becomes a sin when you give in to it. Martin Luther said, "You cannot keep birds from flying over your head but you can keep them from building a nest in your hair." You can keep the Devil from suggesting thoughts, but you can choose not to dwell or act on them."[11] What is temptation? It is a cause for or something that comes into one's life to entice or lure the person to sin against God. 1 Cor. 10:13 "There hath no temptation taken you but such as is common to man: but God is faithful, who will not suffer you to be tempted above that ye are able; but will with the temptation also make a way to escape, that ye may be able to bear it. God is so good, for He will always make a way out of temptation for us. When Cain was about to kill Abel God spoke to Cain that sin was lying at his door and Cain should rule over it. God has given us a will so it is up to us to bring our wills under the will of God or the enemy will control our wills. Cain allowed the enemy to control his will. Gen.4:6-7 "And the Lord said unto Cain, Why art thou wroth? And why is thy countenance fallen? If thou doest well, shalt thou not be accepted? And if thou doest not well, sin lieth at the door. And unto thee shall be his desire, and thou shalt rule over it." When a believer is to enter temptation, the Spirit of God will caution such a person but usually the person may not listen and get into it and sin against God. God has given us a will so it is up to us to rule over temptation or rule over sin. No one will be able to do that for you. You have to overcome sin or the desire of sin will rule over you. When you sin against God, the next thing that the enemy will bring in is guilt and fear. If such a person does not take care she or he may enter deep into sin and continue to sin against God. When you sin please be bold and come before God to confess your sin and repent, for God will forgive you. Let me give you some of the things that the enemy may use to tempt you. If you are a man then the enemy will let you have a lust for women that if you do not take care your lust will turn into having sex with any woman that may give in to your sexual desires. Another thing which the enemy will use to tempt many Christians is money. The enemy will put you in abject poverty that if you do not take care you and your family will become homeless. When the enemy is able to place you in such a situation then the enemy will come in to tempt you with money. You need money so if you do not take care you will find yourself in doing things that you are not suppose to do as a Child of God. The enemy may get you into illicit drug selling, illicit sex, and any illicit thing that may get you money. Looking at 1 Tim. 6:7-10 "For we brought nothing into this world, and it is certain we can carry nothing out. And having food and raiment let us be therewith content. But they that will be rich fall into temptation and a snare, and into many foolish and hurtful lusts, which drown men in destruction and perdition. For the love of money is the root of all evil: which while some coveted after, they have erred from the faith, and pierced themselves through with many sorrows." The love of money may lead one to kill to get the money. Satan is very cunning for he will always bring in so many evil things together just for the destruction of humankind The love of money may cause someone to steal, and while stealing may kill someone in the process. So Satan can combine greed, murder and theft together to achieve his goal, the destruction of humankind. In the Church, some ministers and elders will do what its takes to control the Church finances. They will dip the hands into the Church coffers without thinking that it is God's money for God's work. Allow the Spirit of God to take absolute control of your life, so that you will not give in to the enticement, and ways of the enemy. Let me give you an example, you know very well that this beautiful lady in your Church has a husband, but the enemy will let you covet after her in so much that you cannot dismiss the thought of having a good sex with her. Let me tell you the enemy uses your mind as the battle ground. If you do not dismiss that thought and it sinks into your heart, then you will make the attempt to get this married lady. If she is not strong in the Lord, she may fall for your diabolical tactics and may break her marriage.

5. **Hindrance:** Another work of the enemy is to hinder the believer in every area of life. Satan and his forces will hinder you so that you will never prosper. 1 Thess. 2:18 "Wherefore we would have come unto you, even I Paul, once and again; but Satan hindered us." If Satan hindered Paul, then the enemy could hinder any child of God. The enemy hinders the prayers of Christians, just to frustrate them and to cause them to lose faith in God. If you do not get your prayer answer do not lose heart, but you need to check your walk with God. If you are walking worthy of the vocation of your calling then just exercise patient for God will show up. Daniel, a man greatly beloved, prayed and fasted but his prayer was hindered for twenty-one days. If Satan could hinder the prayers of Daniel then, he can hinder your prayers too. Do not give up and persevere for God will show up. Dan.10:10-14 "And, behold, an hand touched me, which set me upon my knees and upon the palms of my hands. And he said unto me, O Daniel, a man greatly beloved, understand the words that I speak unto thee, and stand upright: for unto thee am I now sent, And when he had spoken this word unto me, I stood trembling. Then said he unto me, Fear not, Daniel: for from the first day that thou didst set thine heart to understand, and to chasten thyself before thy God, thy words were heard, and I am come for thy words. But the prince of the kingdom of Persia withstood me one and twenty days: but, lo, Michael, one of the chief princes, came to help me; and I remained there with the kings of Persia. Now I am come to make thee understand what shall befall thy people in the latter days: for yet the vision is for many days." Daniel was praying to seek the face of God concerning what was going to happen to his people, the Israelites in the latter days, but Satan gathered all his forces to hinder the answer to Daniel's

prayer. The kingdom of Persian stands for Satanic Kingdom. Satan has his own kingdom and he is campaigning day and night to get followers into this horrific kingdom. Satan uses intimidation, fear lust, enticement and money to get many people into his kingdom, which is mark for doom. Satan and his demonic forces will not only hinder your prayers but any good thing that seems to come your way will be hindered. These demonic forces will hinder you from getting a good job so that your financial situation can be improved. We need to pray effectively for breakthrough in the area of finances, or Satan will do his best to keep us in poverty. 2 Pet.1:3-4 "According as his divine power hath given unto us all things that pertain unto life and godliness, through the knowledge of him that hath called us to glory and virtue: whereby are given unto us exceeding great and precious promises: that by these ye might be partakers of the divine nature, having escaped the corruption that is in the world through lust." The divine power of God is there to give to us everything that we should need in this life. The enemy is so crafty that he will not let us know that God's power is there to give us things that we need in this life. We have to know it, believe it and pray about it and live it. For lack of knowledge my people perish. It is the divine power that is propelling us to live a godlily life. We need not to fall into the trap of the enemy just like that for the divine power of God keeps us from sinning. It is this divine power that has helped us to escape the corruption of this world. Satan will use every means to hinder us from getting the blessings of God. A close friend or sibling may do something nasty to you but you have to learn to forgive or Satan will let your blessings be hindered due to the unforgiving spirit working in you. Looking at Psalm 84: 11 "For the Lord God is a sun and a shield: the Lord will give grace and glory: no good thing will he withhold from them that walk uprightly." The Lord God is a sun means, God is the source of our light and we will not walk in darkness if we walk with God. Even in our darkness, the light of God will shine for us. The Lord God is a shield, means God is the protector of those who walk with Him. This is a divine protection, which shield us from all the fiery darts of Satan. The only condition is for us walk uprightly, that is to walk in the vocation of our calling or abiding by the Word of God. Then God will give us good things, any good thing that we need, good job, good home with good kids, long life, wellbeing and prosperity. We need to pray for God to clear any hindrances or traps set by Satan.

6. **Poverty:** Poverty is defined by Webster Dictionary as the state of one who lacks a usual or socially acceptable amount of money or material possessions. For instance at the time of writing, in the United States of America, if the annual income of a family of four is $ 23,000 then, that family is on the poverty line. Looking at Lam. 1: 9-10 "Her filthiness is in her skirts; she remembereth not her last end; therefore she came down wonderfully; she

has no comforter, O Lord, behold my affliction: for the enemy hath magnified himself. The adversary hath spread out his hand upon all her pleasant things:" This was a lamentation over Israel, as the people sin against the God of Israel, this allow the enemy (Satan) to magnified himself over the Israelites and spread his hand over all the their pleasant things. Therefore, the Israelites were stricken with poverty and were also taken into captivity. This means God does not tolerate sin. We need to live right with God and believe in His Word and we will be able to live a prosperous life. If we allow the enemy to spread his hand over our finances, then he will keep us below the poverty level and sink us in deep debt. We need to pray and break the chain of poverty over our life. In the name of Jesus, I pray in the anointing of the Holy Spirit to break any chain of poverty in your life. The Bible declares in Psalm 112: 3 "Wealth and riches shall be in his house;" so I declare wealth and riches to be in your house and the blessings of Abraham to be your portion in the land of the living. May the Blood of Jesus Christ that speaks better things than the blood of Abel, speaks well being, health, prosperity, wealth and riches into your life and your family. May you be blessed like never before in the name of Jesus. Amen. Our Heavenly Father is prepared to see to the well being of his children therefore we should be rest assure that our God will provide. I will like to point out something that is very important. There is a plan and purpose or reason for everything that God will do in your life. God does not bless one with financial overflow for such to be pompous, wicked and do not care about the work of God, the pastor, the poor and needy. God will bless you financially if you are prepared to allow God to direct you how to use the financial blessing. There are ministers who are using any means to get money, therefore be careful how you spend your money on ministers. Please I will advise you to cater for those ministers in your local church before any other. Looking at Josh. 1: 8 "This book of the law shall not depart out of thy mouth; but thou shalt meditate therein day and night, that thou mayest observe to do according to all that is written there in: for then thou shalt make thy way prosperous, and then thou shalt have good success." There is a way to have a good success and this is the Bible way. We as Christians need to read the Bible daily and meditate upon the Word. Then we should be prepared to daily apply the Word of God to our lives. We need to listen to God and God will show us what to do to be prosperous. May be you do not know how to listen to God then you will need my first book entitled "Effective Prayers" published by Xlibris Corporation. You will know how to hear from God for we are worshiping the God who spoke to Abraham, Isaac, David, Peter and Paul. God is still speaking today. We as Christians should not tolerate poverty in our lives for it is the work of the enemy to keep us poor so that he may be able to waive our faith in God. God is prepared to show us what to do so that we can be prosperous. Let us look at Isaiah 48:17-18 "Thus saith the Lord, thy Redeemer, the Holy One of Israel; I am the Lord thy God which teacheth thee to profit, which leadeth thee by the way that thou shouldest go. O that thou hadest hearkened to my commandments! Then had thy peace been as a river and thy righteousness as the waves of the sea." Let us start learning how to hear from God, for it is the will of God to teach us what to do to lead a profitable and fulfilled life in this world. I am from a poor village in Ghana, and born to poor parents so I know what it means to be poor. I am trusting in God to taste His riches. Looking at Psalm 112:1-4 "Praise ye the Lord. Blessed is the man that feareth the Lord, that delighteth greatly in his commandments. His seed shall be mighty upon the earth: the generation of the upright shall be blessed. Wealth and riches shall be in his house; and his righteousness endureth forever. Unto the upright there ariseth light in the darkness: he is gracious and full of compassion, and righteous." I believe God is watching over His Word to perform it. I reverend the Lord and delight in His Word therefore my children are going to be great on earth. Wealth and riches will be in my house. I need to listen to know what God wants me to do and show me how to get wealth and riches in my house. How to use the wealth and riches when the time comes. I believe I have to listen to God to know what to do with the wealth and riches that will come into my house. It is the will of God to make us prosperous. When God make us prosperous, He expects us to use this wealth for spreading the Gospel and bringing many people out of the darkness into His marvelous light. Do not forget, your Pastor, God ministers and the work of God when God blesses you. You need to worship God not only with your spirit, soul and body but with your substances or whatever God has blessed you with. Poverty should not be entertained in our life, for it brings in debt, frustration, depression, confusion, identity crisis, homelessness and many more. As Christians, we need to listen to God, work hard and know how to manage our finances to be at least above the poverty level. How then can we get out of poverty? First we need to pay our tithes and offering to the local Church. Looking at Malachi 3: 6-11 "For I am the Lord, I change not; therefore ye sons of Jacob are not consumed. Even from the days of your fathers ye are gone away from my ordinances, and have not kept them. Return unto me, and I will return unto you, saith the Lord of hosts. But ye said, Wherein shall we return? Will a man rob God? Yet ye have robbed me. But ye said, Wherein have we robbed thee? In tithes and offerings. Ye are cursed with a curse: for ye have robbed me even this whole nation. Bring ye all the tithes into the storehouse, that there may be meat in mine house, and prove me now herewith, saith the Lord of hosts, if I will not open you the windows of heaven, and pour you out a blessing, that there shall not be room enough to receive it. And I will rebuke the devourer for your sakes, and he shall not destroy the fruits of your ground; neither shall your vine cast her fruit before the time in the field, saith the Lord of hosts. To be frank I am the first person to rob God for I have not been paying my tithes. I made a promise from today that I will pay my tithes in order to receive the blessings of God. God is telling us that He has not changed for He is the same yesterday, today and tomorrow. God bless Abraham for Abraham paid his tithes, so God is prepared to bless His children of today if they will pay their tithes. The children of God sin against God when we do not pay our tithes. We rob God and we turn away from Him. God wants us to return to Him with our whole heart and to pay our tithes. We are doubly curse if we do not pay our tithes. Curses of poverty and debt will be knocking at our doors if we do not pay our tithes. God wants us to return to Him and pay our tithes and prove Him to see if He will not open the windows of heaven to bless us in such a way that we cannot contain the blessings. God will also rebuke Satan for our sake so that the devil will not be able to destroy our blessings, health and properties. The next thing to do if we want to receive the abundance of God is to minister to God's people. Looking at 1Corin. 9:13-14 "Do ye not know that they which minister about holy things live of the things of the temple? And they which wait at the altar are partakers with the altar? Even so hath the Lord ordained that they which preach the gospel should live of the gospel." This is something ordained by our Lord Jesus Christ that the pastor who preaches the gospel should make a living of the gospel. If you see a pastor who is financially poor this means the congregation is not taking good care of the pastor so the whole congregation will be poor. If the members of a congregation want to come out of financial difficulties, then they should start paying their tithes and next take a good care of their pastor and God will open the windows of heaven to bless the congregation. Aside from the good salary that the Church will give to the pastor, they should bless the pastor's wife on mother's day, bless the pastor on father's day and do appreciation service at least once a year for the pastor. Please do this and you will see the blessings of God in every area of your life. Another thing that will take us out of poverty is to start putting money into God's work. If there is a building fund for the local Church, then you should do well to give your quota. We should also help with the mission fund. The next thing to do is to minister to the saints. If you are a well to do person in the Church, then if there are other members who are struggling financially then do your best to give a helping hand. Looking at Heb. 6:10 "For God is not unrighteous to forget your work and labour of love, which ye have shewed toward his name, in that ye have ministered to the saints, and do minister." We need to help the saints or Christians who are struggling financially. Like, we always say it is better to teach those struggling financially how to fish rather than to give them a basket of fish. When we do this God is telling us He is not unrighteous to forget what we have done for our fellow Christians. God will not forget our work and labor of love which we have shown towards his name, for ministering to other Christians. If there are widows and orphans in our midst then we need to minister to them too. As we minister to the poor, needy, orphans and widows, then God is also going to bless the work of our hands. Poverty is a disease so we should walk in faith for wealth and riches to be our portion in the land of the living. The next thing that I want to talk about can be found in Proverbs 13:22, which states "A good man will leave an inheritance to his children's children but the wealth of the wicked is laid for the just." Who is the good person the bible is talking about? It is the person, who knows the Lord Jesus Christ. Therefore, every Christian is to leave an inheritance to his/her children's children. What kind of inheritance is the Word talking about? I will say heavenly inheritance and earthly inheritance. They are both needed for our children's children. Heavenly inheritance, for God wants us to have godly seeds, that is help our children to know Jesus Christ as their Savior and Lord. We are to teach our children how to walk with God. The next inheritance is earthly, which is wealth and riches. Looking at Proverbs 13:22 b "and the wealth of the sinner is laid up for the just." This shows us the inheritance here is earthly, which are houses, wealth and riches. Looking at Proverbs 19:14 "Houses and riches are the inheritance from the fathers: and a prudent wife is from the Lord." In Ghana, there is an adage that, so far as I have taken care of my child for his/her teeth to grow, then my child should take care of me, when my teeth are out. Which means, my children are to take care of me when I grow old. This is not what the Bible says. If I am to leave an inheritance to my children's children, then how should my children turn around to take care of me. I believe this is the main reason why there is a lot of poverty in Ghana. Instead of helping our children to stand firm in the Lord Jesus, in health and finances, we the older generation are draining our children. If we want to see our children prospering then we have to live according to the Word of God and leave an inheritance for our children's children. We have a long way to go for it is not only for our children but their children too. I was giving a teaching about living an inheritance to our children's children, and an elder in the church stood against what I was teaching, saying the inheritance the bible is talking about is heavenly and not earthly. I did not want to fight over interpretation of the Scriptures, so I let it go. If we look at the second part of Proverb 13:22, the Word says "and the wealth of the sinner is laid up for the just." If the second part of the same verse is talking about wealth, then I think God want us to leave wealth, houses and riches as inheritance for our children and their children. You may say how can it be in this difficult economy, but with God all things are possible.

Chapter Six

The Love of the world

7. **The Love of the world:** The love of the world is at enmity to Christ Jesus and anything godly. Looking at James 4:4 Ye adulterers and adulteresses, know ye not that the friendship of the world is enmity with God? Whosoever therefore will be a friend of the world is the enemy of God. This simply means as soon as you become friendly to the world then you become an adulterer, which is a serious crime before God. Let me give you an example a child of God who loves watching play boy, naked sexy videos, going to disco, and places to peep, cease to be a child of God. Unless such a person confesses his/her sins and repents to be restored to God. Another example is a child of God who gets himself/ herself involve in bribery and corruption at work place also has love the world and needs to confess and repent. A child of God should also be careful the type of music she/he listens to. Most of the worldly music are not healthy for the Christian growth as the words are trash and has no inspiration. We need to dress modestly and should not allow the world to dictate what kind of hair or dress to put on. "Nothing is more explicit than this, nothing is more commanding, authoritative and more exacting. "Love not the world." Nothing is more offensive to God, nothing is more criminal, more abominable, violative of the most sacred relationship of the soul with God. "Adulteresses"—purity gone and shame and illicit intercourse exist. Friendship of the world is Heaven's greatest enemy. The world is one of the enemies which must be fought and conquered on the way to heaven." For this is the love of God, that we keep his commandments; and his commandments are not grievous. For whatsoever is born of God overcometh the world, and this is the victory that overcometh the world, even our faith. Who is he that overcometh the world, but he that believe that Jesus is the Son of God?"[12]

Looking at 1 Joh. 2:15-16 "Love not the world, neither the things that are in the world. If any man loves the world, the love of the Father is not in him. For all that is in the world, the lust of the flesh, the lust of the eyes, and the pride of life, is not of the Father, but is of the world. Christians have to be careful for it is easy to be attracted to the things of the world without being aware of your surroundings, or what is going on. The love of the world is grievous and abominable in the sight of God. The lust of the fresh, the lust of the eyes and the pride of life are the same three things, which the enemy used to get Adam and Eve to sin against God. Let us look at everyone of them, and see how Satan used it to entice Adam and Eve to sin against God. Let us look at the temptation of Adam and Eve at Gen. 3:1-6 Now the serpent (Satan) was more subtil than any beast of the field which the Lord God had made. And he said unto the woman, Yea, hath God said, Ye shall not eat of every tree of the garden? (Satan twisted God's word to deceive Eve.) And the woman said unto the serpent, We may eat of the fruit of the trees of the garden: But of the fruit of the tree which is in the midst of the garden, God hath said, Ye shall not eat of it, neither shall ye touch it, lest ye die. *(Eve should not have enter into dialogue with Satan but cast him out of her imagination. God has also given us a free will to choose to be on His side or reject His offer.)* And the serpent said unto the woman, Ye shall not surely die*: (this is a total lie from the bottom of hell.)* For God doth know that in the day ye eat thereof, then your eyes shall be opened, and ye shall be as gods, knowing good and evil.*(This is the pride of life, wanting to be something that you are not supposed to be. Eve wanted to be like god. There are so many people out there who want to be like god. It is good to get a PhD but if the motive behind it is wrong then you need to change your attitude. It is good to be a celebrity but if you are a celebrity who does not want to do anything with ordinary people then you have to change your attitude.)*And when the woman saw that the tree was good for food, and that it was pleasant to the eyes, *(this is the lust of the eyes, so we have to be very careful what we watch, if you watch sexy films and videos, it is easy to be involved in sexual immorality)*, and a tree to be desire to make one wise,*(the lust of the flesh, desiring something that is not yours)*, she took of the fruit thereof, and eat, and gave also unto her husband with her; and he did eat. (italics mine). Adam and Eve loved the world, which belongs to the prince of the air and this brought an enmity between God and the human race. Let us give thanks to God for He did not left us in that state but sent His only Son Jesus Christ to die on the cross for us so that through the sacrificial death of Jesus Christ we can be reconcile to Him if only we believe. God has given us a will so it is up to us to accept what God has done through Jesus Christ or reject this offer.

"The Gospel is represented as a training school in which to deny worldly desires is one part of its curriculum. "For the grace of God that bringeth salvation hath appeared to all men, teaching us, that denying ungodliness and worldly lust, we should live soberly, righteously and godly, in this present world; looking for that blessed hope, and the glorious appearing of the great God and our Saviour Jesus Christ; who gave himself for us, that he might redeem us from all iniquity, and purify unto himself a peculiar people, zealous of good works." There is something somewhere in the world which makes it a deadly foe to the salvation of Christ and poisons us against heaven. What is "this world," which so effectually alienates us from heaven and puts us by virtue of our relation to it and in flagrant enmity to God, and friendship to which violates our wedding vow to God, whose love is enmity to God, whose friendship is criminal to the most abominable and utmost degree? What is it? "The world, the lust of the flesh, the lust of the eyes, the pride of life." What are they? The world includes the whole mass of men alienated from God, and therefore hostile to the cause of Christ. It involves worldly affairs, the aggregate of things earthly, the whole circle of earthly goods, endowments, riches, advantages, pleasure, and pursuits, which although hollow, frail and fleeting, stir desire, seduce from God, and are obstacles to the cause of Christ. The divorce or torn relation between heaven and earth, between God and His creatures, finds its expression in the term, "the world."[13]

What is lust? It is an intense pleasure or desire for something. For instance, someone may have a lust for power, or a lust for sexual desire. The enemy will come in with inferiority complex, and a person may feel insecure, so the only way out is for such a person to have a lust for power. In a marriage, a husband who may feel insecure, may lust for power by suppressing the wife or even physically and morally abusing the wife. A wife who may feel insecure will also show up by insulting the husband or morally abuse the husband. In such a marriage if nothing is done, it may end up in divorce.

a) Lust of the flesh: It is a state whereby one desires something for the flesh or the body, that, such a person may do anything to get what he/she is seeking for. If the person is a man, then he may have a lust for sexual immorality and he may be in bed with any women who may give him the chance. If this desire is not control a person may even get involve in masturbation if he does not get any woman to have sex with. Masturbation is an ungodly desire which should not be entertained by any child of God. What is masturbation? Merriam Webster defined masturbation as an erotic stimulation of especially one's own genital organs commonly resulting in orgasm and achieved by manual or other bodily contact exclusive of sexual intercourse, by instrumental manipulation, occasionally by sexual fantasies, or by various combination of these agencies. This act of masturbation is lust of the flesh and should not be entertained by any child of God. A woman may also have a lust for sex that she may go to bed with any man that, comes into her life. If such a life is not control, such a person will turn out to be a nymphomaniac. A person may have a lust for money, so she/he will do anything to get rich, either by selling of drugs, or involving in illicit sex. The enemy is so cunning and crafty that Satan will use deception, flattery and any means to get people to lust for things that are not necessary. Satan is not afraid of anyone, except the person who is in Jesus Christ and walking worthy of the vocation of his or her calling. This means you are abiding by the Word of God. The lust of the flesh may cause a person to desire for something that does not belong to him/her. Someone may lust after someone's wife that he may do everything to get this woman if the woman is not a child of God.

b) Lust of the eyes: This is the eyes that look and desire for things which does not belong to him/her. The eyes are the gateway to the body and it opens the door for the lust of the flesh. The eyes may lust for something and the flesh will just agree to it, so most of the time, the lust of the eyes and the lust of the flesh are like twins that do everything together. We have to be careful what we watch as Christians for we may get addicted to something which may not be good for a Child of God. For instance if you like watching sexy films or videos, you may be addicted to it, and which is bad for a Child of God. If you like watching pornographic pictures, then the enemy may get you going to places like peeping, where you are not supposed to go as a Child of God. The lust of the eyes may entice you to do things that are contrary to walking worthy of the vocation of your calling.

c) Pride of life: What is pride? Merriam Webster defines pride as the quality or state of being proud. This is the desire for something that will make you feel proud for achieving it. The point is if you are a Child of God, then what ever you will achieve is not by your wisdom, strength or power, but by the Spirit of the Living God. Looking at Phil. 4: 13 "I can do all things through Christ which strengtheneth me." We are able to achieve something good for ourselves but we must know that it is the power of Christ that helps us to achieve everything in this world. Anytime we think it is by our strength might and intelligence than the pride of life has kicked in. It is good to get a PhD but if we want to get it to show to the world how smart we are then we have allow the pride of life to override us. If you know it is Christ who has given you the wisdom for your PhD then you have recognized the source of your wisdom and it is not the pride of life.

d) The love of the world: The divine warning against the course of the world, against the fashion of the world and against the spirit of the world, finds its solution in the fact that the devil is directing the world's course, the devil is creating the world's spirit, and the devil is cutting the pattern of the world's fashion. The touch of the world pollutes because Satan's fingers are in its touch. Its desires are deadly and heaven-quenching because Satan kindles its desires. The world and its things are contraband in the Christian warfare because Satan is the ruler of the world and the administrator of its affairs.[14]

8. **Unforgiving:** It is a state whereby one is not able to pardon another person for the horrible things that this person did to him/her. I love the way Col Wash of Hermitage High defines unforgiving, which is choosing to stay trapped in a jail cell of bitterness serving time for someone's crime (Merriam Webster Dictionary). It is a choice to forgive. You either choose to forgive the person who has done you wrong, or you allow unforgiving spirit to take hold of you. We need not only to forgive but forget. If you do not forgive, you will allow the enemy to come into your arena to attack you with bitterness and jealousy when you see the person you are holding grudge against is doing well or prospering in life. You may be a young lady who is not able to forgive your father or a family member who raped you when you were young. I bear your pain but please do forgive or you will be holding up your own blessings. The enemy plays on our intelligence to keep us in bitterness against someone who has offended us. The enemy will tell you it is a sign of weakness to forgive and the one you are forgiving will take your leniency to be your weakness. Please do as the Bible says and leave the outcome to God. God will reward you for forgiving the person who did horrible things to you. May be someone shot you with a gun, and because of that you are paralyzed and sitting in a wheel chair, consume with bitterness and revenge. I can feel your pain but the only thing I can say is pleased in the name of our Lord Jesus Christ do forgive. Looking at Matth. 18:21-22 "Then came Peter to him, and said, Lord, how oft shall my brother sin against me, and I forgive him? till seven times? Jesus said unto him, I say not unto thee, until seven times, but until seventy times seven." Peter wanted to take the easy way, that is, if someone sin against me for seven times, it would be easy to count, but Jesus said seventy times seven, which is four hundred and ninety times, which will not be easy to count. Jesus is telling us to forgive for vengeance belongs to God. Any Child of God should be able to forgive, as Stephen did when he was stoned to death by his accusers. Looking at Acts 7: 54-59 "When they heard these things, they were cut to the heart, and they gnashed on him with their teeth. But he, being full of the Holy Ghost, looked up steadfastly into heaven, and saw the glory of God, and Jesus standing on the right hand of God, And said, Behold, I see the heavens opened, and the Son of man standing at the right hand of God. Then they cried out with a loud voice, and stopped their ears, and ran upon him with one accord, And cast him out of the city, and stoned him; and the witness laid down their clothes at a young man's feet, whose name was Saul. And they stoned Stephen, calling upon

God, and saying, Lord Jesus, receive my spirit. And he kneeled down, and cried with a loud voice, Lord, lay not this sin to their charge. And when he has said this, he fell asleep." This is Christianity, when at the point of death, you are able to forgive those who killed you. In this modern time, if someone shot at you, and at the point of death with the gun wounds, if you are able to forgive then you are a genuine Christian. Saul who watched the clothes of the perpetrators as they stoned Stephen to death was as guilty as those who stone him. Stephen was able to forgive them so it was not laid to the charge of Saul. Saul turned out to be Paul, and I believe it was because Stephen was able to forgive him. When we are able to forgive, then God is not going to hold that sin against the one who did it. When we do not forgive, then the person will be held accountable. If we do not forgive, we will also be locked up with bitterness, and withhold our blessings. Looking at John 20:21-23 "Then said Jesus to them again, Peace be unto you: as my Father hath sent me, even so send I you. And when he had said this, he breathed on them, and saith unto them, Receive ye the Holy Ghost: Whose soever sins ye remit, they are remitted unto them, and whosesoever sins ye retain, they are retained." Jesus Christ has given us (Christians) the power to forgive sins or to retain sins. If we forgive those who hurt us, they are forgiven but if we do not then they will be held accountable for what they did to us. The central message of Christianity is forgiveness. Jesus died on the cross, so that anyone who will believe will be washed of his/her sins and will be forgiven and be reconciled to God. It is not easy to forgive, for instance if one was a witness to someone shooting her mother or father to death. But when the Spirit of God comes and lives in us then we will be able to forgive through the Spirit of God living in us. How does the Spirit of God come and live in us? When you accept Jesus as your personal Savior and Lord, then God sends his Spirit to live in you. It is the Spirit of God that can give you God's love to love others especially your partner. Looking at Rom. 5:5 "And hope maketh not ashamed: because the love of God is shed abroad in our hearts by the Holy Ghost which is give to us." Therefore, through the power of the Holy Spirit, Christians are able to love others with the love of God. Christians are also able to forgive through the power of the Holy Spirit. A Christian who is not able to forgive has a long way to go. Such a person is still holding on to his/her own will and has not surrender his/her will to God. We should allow the Holy Spirit to work in us so that we will be able to forgive others who have offended us. What about if your wife or husband is caught in adultery? You are supposed to forgive, and you can do this if you allow the Spirit of God to work in your heart to take away any pain and hurt.

9. **STEPS TO FORGIVE:** "Leslie D. Weatherhead once said that the forgiveness of God is the most therapeutic idea in the whole world. Psychological adjustment is wonderful, and we

need more of it. But nothing in all the earth which man can do, can ever satisfy the human need for forgives. It is at the heart of human problem. Any treatment of the human dilemma that ignores the need for forgiveness at the hands of God is superficial. It leaves the deeper needs of the human spirit untouched and unhealed."[15] The central theme of Christianity is forgiveness. Jesus Christ died on the cross so that our sins will be forgiven us and we will be reconciled to God. Therefore every child of God should be able to forgive as God has forgiven us. "Therefore if any man be in Christ, he is a new creature: the old things are passed away; behold, all things are new. And all things are of God, who hath reconciled us to himself by Jesus Christ, and hath given us the ministry of reconciliation. (2 Cor. 5: 17-18). Forgiveness is the first step of rebuilding a broken relationship. "Relationships are always worth restoring. Because life is all about learning how to love, God wants us to value relationships and make the effort to maintain them instead of discarding them whenever there is a rift, a hurt, or a conflict. In fact, the Bible tells us that God has given us the ministry of restoring relationships.[16] Therefore, the first step is to know that forgiveness is the central theme of Christianity. God through his Son, Jesus Christ has forgiven us our sins and we should in the same way forgive those who have offended us. Learn to forgive yourself and you will be able to forgive others. Sometimes, we lock ourselves in bitterness, pain and anger and also feel it was our fault such a nasty thing happened to us. It is not your fault, so do not lock yourself up in bitterness and do forgive yourself, and know that you are worthy in the eyes of God. Secondly, we should allow the Holy Sprit to search our hearts and accept the forgiveness that God has given to us through his Son Jesus Christ. "Augustine felt pretty good about himself when he compared his morality to that of his fellows at the University of Carthage. He thought he was a good, pure, noble, young man. Then Augustine said, "One day Jesus of Nazareth cross my path, and I saw what a terrible mess I'd made." In the white light of Jesus' character, we see ourselves for who we really are. Those horizontal comparisons comfort us, while a comparison with Christ convicts us.[17] If there is a grudge or some form of enmity between you and another person, then you can never love this person unless you forgive the person. We can forgive for we are new creatures, the old person who cannot forgive is gone. The next step is start praying for the person you want to forgive. Note that God was able to reconcile us to himself after forgiving us of our sins. God has also given to us the ministry of reconciliation, therefore we do not only forgive but reconcile. The next and final step is to love the one who hurts us. This can only be done through prayers. We should learn to forgive. We should not allow the spirit of unforgiving to consume us and put us in the cage of bitterness, jealousy, and frustration which will slow down any progress that we are making in life. Looking at Matt. 6:9-13 "After this manner therefore pray ye: Our Father which art in heaven, Hallowed be thy name, Thy kingdom come, Thy will be done on earth, as it is in heaven, Give us this day our daily bread. And forgive us our debts, as we forgive our debtors. And lead us not into temptation, but deliver us from evil: For thy is the kingdom, and the power, and the glory, forever. Amen." In our Lord's prayer, what I am concerned about is "forgive us our debts as we forgive our debtors", there is a condition for us to be forgiven our debts or sins and this condition is for us to forgive our debtors. Therefore, if you are not going to forgive someone when she/he offends or sin against you then do not expect God also to forgive you, your sins when you sin against Him. Learn to forgive so that God will also forgive you of your sins. Another thing you can do is to buy a very simple gift and give it to the person. And if you are not on talking terms then start talking to the person. Sometimes if there is a need to bring a third person, like you pastor into the situation you can do that, so that the matter can be settled amicably. Do forgive for unforgiving is a burden to carry.

Riotous Living: The enemy is so crafty and smart that he is able to outwit anyone who is not alert of his tactics. The story about a son who spent his part of his inheritance on riotous living is found in Luke 15: 11-32 "And he said, A certain man had two sons: And the younger of them said to his father, Father give me the portion of goods that falleth to me. And he divided unto them his living. And not many days after the younger son gathered all together, and took his journey into a far country, and there wasted his substance with riotous living. And when he had spend all, there arose a mighty famine in that land; and he began to be in want. And he went and joined himself to a citizen of that country; and he sent him into his fields to feed swine. And he would fain have filled his belly with the husks that the swine did eat: and no man gave unto him. And when he came to himself, he said, How many hired servants of my father's have bread enough and to spare, and I perish with hunger! I will arise and go to my father, and I will say unto him, Father, I have sinned against heaven, and before thee, And I am no more worthy to be called thy son: make me as one of thy hired servants. And he arose, and came to his father. But when he was yet great way off, his father saw him and had compassion, and ran, and fell on his neck, and kissed him. And the son said unto him, Father I have sinned against heaven, and in thy sight, and am no more worthy to be called thy son. But the father said to his servant, Bring forth the best robe, and put it on him; and put a ring on his hand, and shoes on his feet: And bring hither the fatted calf, and kill it; and let us eat, and be merry: For this my son was dead, and is alive again; he was lost and is found. And they begun to make merry. Now his elder son was in the field: and as he came and drew nigh the house, he heard musick and dancing. And he called one of the servants, and asked what these things meant. And he said unto him thy brother is come; and thy father hath killed the fatted calf, because he hath received him safe and sound. And he was angry, and would not go in: therefore came his father out, and intreated him. And he answering said to his father, Lo, these many years do I serve thee, neither transgressed I at any time thy commandments: and yet that never gavest me a kid, that I might, make merry with my friends: But as soon as this thy son was come, which hath devoured thy living with harlots, thou hath killed for him the fatted calf. And he said unto him, Son thou art ever with me, and all that I have is thine. It was meet that we should make merry, and be glad: for this thy brother was dead, and is alive again; and was lost, and is found." The Bible is so relevant to our present time, for there are so many vagabonds and prodigal sons in our time, who are hustling their parents. The younger son was so selfish, and disrespectful, that he would not wait till the death of his father to get the part of his inheritance. This younger son asked for the portion of his inheritance while the father was still alive. He was saying, father I wished you were dead! The behavior of this child was so uncouth, barbaric, and uncivilized. The father was so matured and benevolent, that he did not question his child but gave the portion of his inheritance to him. The father understood the difficulties of life, he knew what it meant to hustle and work hard to be successful in this life. This was a very successful man whose younger child was disrespectful and cared not what this life holds for him in the future. This young man did not know that your present decisions and actions would determine your future. He had no experience in this life and he was too childish. The father knew something that the child did not know, so the father allowed the son to have his own way and to get life lessons and experiences. The son traveled into a far country, where he would not be under any parental influence or control. This younger son had never work or experience any hardships in this life, and he did not know how many people were just making ends meet by working two or three jobs. He knew nothing about the hustles of life. He got his bounty free of charge and did not know how to take care of his wealth and riches. He started living anyhow and wasted his substance on riotous living. He misappropriated his riches and wealth on reckless and pompous living. He had a high standard of living without thinking of how to save or invest for the future. He lost all he had. He had nothing to hold on to and started to feel the pains and reality of life. He was in needs or wants, where to lay his head, how to pay his rent, put food on the table, and the clothes to wear. He was facing the difficulties of life and he was in need of the basic things in life; which are food, shelter and clothing. He started to look for a job and worked as a menial worker in the field, (which means out of the city) feeding pigs. A rich man's son working in a countryside feeding pigs and eating what the pigs ate. This was a very horrible experience. Thanks be to God, for this foolish son came to his sense, which means he became aware of his situation. He decided to do something about it. He said, my father is rich and he has servants working for him. There is more food to eat in the house with leftovers, why should I stay in a foreign country and die of hunger? This young boy decided to do something about his predicament. He decided to go home and said to his father "I have sinned against you and I am not worthy to be your son but hire me as one of your servants". He went back and when he was far off coming to the house, the father saw him and had compassion on him so he ran to hug the son. The son said "I have sinned against you, and I am not worthy to be called your son." The father said to one of his servants "bring the best attire, ring, and shoes and put them on my son. Let us a make a feast, for my son was dead but now he is alive." The father put a ring on the son's finger, which means you are my legal son. The father threw a party for the lost son who had come back alive. The elder son was not around when the younger brother came in. The elder son when he got to the house was not prepared to enter. He was furious for the father had never given him a small cow for him to have a party with friends. The father had to come out to convince him to come in.

Many people are leading a reckless life, they are shopper-phobia and will always be at the Mall shopping. Sometimes they shop for the things they do not need and waste their money. There are people whether they have money or not, they will always spend the weekend in the Mall shopping. There are people who will also eat everything that they see, and they will buy and eat till they cannot breath. They know it is not good for their health but they cannot control their eating habit. There are so many things that we crave for which are not good, some of them are detrimental to our health and we do not even care. Please greediness will not help us so let us cut our coats according to our sizes. We should stop wasting money on reckless living.

Chapter Seven

Murder and Gun Violence

10. Murder and Gun violence: The devil goes about as fierce, as resolute, and as strong as a lion, intent only to destroy, restrained by no sentiments which soften and move human or divine hearts. He has no pity and no sympathy. He is great, but only great in evil. A great intellect, he is driven and inspired by a malignant and cruel heart.[18] Satan is a murderer and his major plan is to kill and destroy the human race. Satan wants to be worshiped and as long as he is not able to achieve his goal, it is his mission to declare war against humanity. Looking at John 8:44 "Ye are of your father the devil, and the lusts of your father ye will do. He was a murderer from the beginning, and abode not in the truth, because there is no truth in him. When he speaketh a lie, he speaketh of his own: for he is a lair, and the father of it." Satan is a murderer and he has declared a war against the human race, with the intent to kill and destroy as many as he can. Satan is also father of lies, he is a lair and does his best to get many people, including some Christians to lie. Satan has assigned some of his agents, evil spirits, demons, and powers of darkness to specific region, state, city or geographic location only to bring in guns, drugs, and violence. In countries where the economy is good, Satan will find pocket areas where poverty prevails and entangle or enslave these areas with drugs, guns, and violence. Solving the problem of gun violence is not an easy thing. Satan and his forces are working around the cloak to make law makers adamant by passing gun laws to get rid of assault weapons and weapons of high capacity of the street. Most of the law makers are members of riffle associations therefore, they love guns and may not like to get rid of the right of the people to bear arms. Prohibition of drugs is another thing, for there are some who believe if drugs are legalize then the violence in the streets will be curbed. They think drugs and guns are twin brothers so if drugs are legalized then the need for guns will not be necessary as most of the gun violence are drug related. To every action, there is a reaction, therefore I personally do not know what will be following drug legalization. May be gun violence will be curb but the rate of suicide and homicide may be increased, as there will be a lot of crazy people roaming the streets. In America, many states have legalized drugs so let wait and see the results in about twenty years of this drug legalization. Satan and his forces will do their best to hook anyone who will avail him/herself on drugs and when one is addicted to the drugs, it becomes difficult for such a person to be free from drug addiction. "Science nowadays has thrown off the yoke of theology: it no longer admits explanations based on divine or diabolic influence…. Eminent teachers have, for a long time, been studying the peculiar neuro-pathological disorders which were formerly considered supernatural in origin. Thanks to their work and the stimulus they have given to contemporary research, that imaginary being, Satan has completely disappeared; his place has been taken, by general consent, by scientific reality.[19] Drug addiction can bring in many mental disorder, which may let those addicted behave in a disorderly manner. No one is born to be a drug addict but the society in which one finds him/herself can breed a group of drug addict. I believe, while we are trying to get rid of guns form our streets we should also find way to address drug and drug addiction. If we get rid of the guns without addressing drugs and drug addiction, there will still be violence on our streets. Satan is the author of confusion, so if we tried to get rid of guns to curb gun violence, Satan will surely bring in another thing, which will instigate or promote violence. Satan is so crafty.

Satan is the author of many incurable diseases and sickness but science has displaced this notion. Satan is so crafty and will cause people to love drugs that are dangerous to their health and will finally get many of those people hook to the drugs. They become addicted and cannot live a single day without the drugs. Many celebrities cannot live without drugs, as most famous musician and actors use drugs to be able to perform well and get the audiences to love them. Many of these celebrities latter find themselves entangle with drugs and Satan moves further to use drug overdose to kill them. Satan final mission is to kill and destroy people and Satan achieves this through gun violence, drugs, suicide and homicide. Like I have said already, Satan's final mission is to kill and he may accomplish this through so many means such as suicide, homicide, drug addiction and so on.

11. **Sexual Immoralities:** One cannot help being a little disturbed by the silence on the subject of the devil that reigns in so much of the so-called "modern" spirituality. The simplest thing is not to speak of it: if one speaks, one seems to smile, and to leave the hearer with the painful impression that we only believe in the devil by way of an easy conformity that does not pretend to depth. And it is doubtless the masterpiece of this master of illusion to pass himself off as non-existent in a world where he so easily gets souls to go the way he wants, without needing to show himself: he has every interest in not doing so. St John of the

Cross, for his part, has no doubts concerning the devil. He knows that he is the "strongest and wiliest of our enemies", and the most "difficult to unmask." He is skilful enough to turn the world and the flesh to his own account, as his two most faithful acolytes. The saint does not hesitate to say that the devil "causes the ruin of a great multitude of religious who set out the life of perfection." Not, let us hope, to their eternal loss, but he prevents them from realizing all the holiness they aim at. Let him smile who will: "There is no human power that can be compared with his, and thus only the divine power suffices to be able to conquer him, and the divine light alone to penetrate his wiles.[20] The devil has blindfolded the world and anyone who gives in to his diabolical tactics. The devil will deceive people to do things that are abominable in the eyes of God. All sorts of sexual immoralities are going on in our society which I believe if our society continues on such path then the wrath of God will come upon our generation. These sexual immoralities are abominable to God, which are:

a. **Homosexuality**: God created us for a purpose so that a man and a woman will come together in a marriage to procreate and have our kind. If this purpose is override then whatever comes in is an abomination to God. Looking at Rom 1: 18-27 and taking it verse by verse; then verse 18 says "For the wrath of God is revealed from heaven against all ungodliness and unrighteousness of men, who hold the truth in unrighteousness;" This means God's anger will come against every person who lives an ungodly and unrighteous life. If you are living an ungodly life it means you are not living according to the Word of God, or the plan and purpose which God has designed for our lives. Living an unrighteous life means you are not living right with God. This means one can go to church and still not living right with God. We have to know Jesus as our personal Savior and Lord then live according to the Word of God to be able to live right with God. Looking at verse 19-20 "Because that which may be known of God is manifest in them; for God hath shewed it unto them. For the invisible things of him from the creation of the world are clearly seen, being understood by the things that are made, even his eternal power and Godhead; so that they are without excuse;" The reason why there is no excuse for those who are living ungodly and unrighteous lives is that these people do not want to retain God in their lives, and they are living as if there is no God and if there is God they do not care but everything that is to be seen of God is manifested in the creation. I think the sun, moon and stars are not just hanging up in space but I believe there is a force that is holding them together. Looking at Psalm 19:1 "The heavens declare the glory of God; and the firmament sheweth his handiwork." Therefore there is a revelation of God in creation. What about the plants, animals, the sea, sea weeds, sea animals, insects, reptiles, different types of fishes and many other things in the world; how do they come into being? These things show there is a God who wants us to live according to His plan and purpose for this life. If anyone decides to live life his/her own way then such a person should be prepared to face the wrath of God if not now then on judgment day. There is a God that is why Psalm 14:1 declares, "The fool hath said in his heart, There is no God." I believe we will not allow Satan to bring in his phony and uncouth behavior to deceive us to say there is no God. Turning the Word to Rom. 1:21 "Because that, when they knew God, they glorified him not as God, neither were thankful; but became vain in their imaginations, and their foolish heart was darkened." The thoughts or what one imagines in the mind get down to the heart and controls the whole person. The rejection of God leads to vain imagination which means the thought process is filled with wicked and vain things which in turn control such a carnal person. In the process the heart also becomes darkened which set such a person under the influence of Satan. Satan can fill such mind with the thoughts of suicide, vengeance, murder, cruelty and violence. Looking at Romans 1:22 "Professing themselves to be wise, they became fools." Many people think, it is by their strength or wisdom which had helped them to make it in this life. Many have study to acquire wisdom to make them think there is no God and everything that they have been able to achieve is through their own ingenuity, wisdom, and strength. The Word of God says you become a fool if you eliminate God in your life. As a Christian, I want you to know that whatever you have been able to achieve in this life in through the power of God. Deut. 8:11-14 "Beware that thou forget not the Lord thy God, in not keeping his commandments, and his judgments, and his statutes, which I command thee this day; Lest when thou hast eaten and art full, and hast built goodly houses, and dwelt therein; And when thy herds and thy flocks multiply, and thy silver and thy gold is multiplied and all that thou hast is multiplied; Then thine heart be lifted up, and thou forget the Lord thy God, which brought thee forth out of the land of Egypt, from the house of bondage." We need to acknowledge what God has done in our lives, as Christians. Being able to live and breath each day is a blessing. We only thing about amassing wealth, riding the best cars and building beautiful mansions, but our lives do not depend on these things. When we seek the kingdom of God and his righteousness then these things will be like fringe benefits, which God will use to bless us. One important thing is that we should not let our heart be lift up, that is becoming, so pompous or arrogant to forget about God, when we are financially, materially and physically blessed. There are some members in the church, who are financially rich and arrogant that in any church meeting, they are bossy and whatever they say should be final. Some members and elders go on to say we are paying the pastor, so the pastor should conform to our standard, what we want, so the pastor is afraid to preach what God has given him/her but will compromise the Word of God and preach what the congregation wants to hear. Really, there are so many people in the church whose behavior needs much to be desire. They listen to the Word of God every day but they do not put the Word into practice. Looking at Deut. 8: 17-18 "And thou say in thine heart, My power and the might of mine hand hath gotten me this wealth. But thou shalt remember the Lord thy God: for it is he that giveth thee power to get wealth, that he may establish his covenant which he sware unto thy fathers, as it is this day." As Christians, we have to know that whatever we are able to achieve in this life is by the grace and power of God. When we trust in the Lord to bless us then we will be careful to take the credit when God bless us. We should not be proud for it is God who has given us the power to get wealth. We usually become proud and boastful when we are well to do financially, thinking our own intelligence or the might of our strength has giving us the breakthrough in the area of finance and well- being. We should note that it is the divine power of God, that has given us wealth, riches, strength and wellbeing. Let us move on to Rom. 1: 23-24 "And changed the glory of the uncorruptible God into an image made like to corruptible man, and to birds, and four footed beast, and creeping things. Wherefore God also gave them up to uncleanness through the lust of their own hearts, to dishonor their own bodies between themselves." When we forsake God then, God will also gave us over to uncleanness and anything disgusting and to do with our bodies things which are abomination before God. As in Rom. 1:26-27 "For this cause God gave them up unto vile affections: for even their women did change the natural use into that which is against nature: And likewise also the men, leaving the natural use of the woman, burned in their lust one toward another; men with men working that which is unseemly, and receiving in themselves that recompence of their error which was meet." Satan will work hard for humankind to rebel against God for what God has put in place for procreation. The man and a woman have to come together in marriage matrimony to reproduce godly children. As many people have decided not to retain God in their mind, God also has given them over to degenerate mind doing things that is not normal, like men having sex with men and women having sex with women which the Bible termed as homosexuality. It is not natural to do such things and it is a great abomination before God. American and European leaders have accepted this act of homosexuality, which is abominable to God. They have not only accepted this detestable sin but doing their best to impose it on the third world countries where, homosexuality is seen as a taboo due to traditions and culture. Let the President of America, Russia, England, France, Germany, and any part of the world accept homosexuality, it does not matter, for it is still an abomination before God, the Almighty. Looking at Rom. 1: 28-32 "And even as they did not like to retain God in their knowledge, God gave them over to a reprobate mind, to do those things which are not convenient; Being filled with all unrighteousness, fornication, wickedness, covetousness, maliciousness; full of envy, murder, debate, deceit, malignity; whisperers, Backbiters, haters of God, despiteful, proud, boasters, inventors of evil things, disobedient to parents, Without understanding, covenant-breakers, without natural affection, implacable, unmerciful; Who knowing the judgment of God, that they which commit such things are worthy of death, not only do the same, but have pleasure in them that do them." There are people who do not want to know anything about God and they think their strength, knowledge and the power of their might and wisdom has gotten them where they are. They think they are smarter than anyone in this world and even smarter than God himself. Therefore God has given them over to a reprobate mind that is they are good for nothing fellows, they have nothing good in their mind. These people do not care about God, and the enemy has taken control over their mind, so they can do all sort of things that are abomination in the sight of God. They are haters of God, boasters, and inventors of evil things. Being haters of God means they do not want to hear anything about God and careless if God even exit. They are boasters which, means they are proud, egocentric, and think everything in this world revolves around them. They do not care about other people and always want to use others to their own advantage. They are inventors of evil thing, which means they are always trying their best to discover new evil ways of doing things. They are good for nothing fellows and do not want to hear or know anything about God. They are without understanding, their view, or point has to be taken, and when they talk, no one is supposed to give an opposite opinion. They are covenant breakers and do not care about a covenant or a promised made. Marriage is a covenant made between a man and woman to be together till death do apart. They do not care about marriage and do not take it to be a covenant made. They can divorce eight times and remarried nine times and do not care, because they are covenant breakers. They are disobedient to parents, and some of them are at logger head with their parents, and do not care about their own parents and any elderly persons. They are without natural affection, which means, the men will not go after women but men. In the same way, the women will not go after men but women. They are homosexual because they do not want anything to do with God or they do not want to retain God in their knowledge. No one is born to be homosexual but only society makes them so. The Bible cautions us that the judgment of God is coming against all those who do such awful acts and not only on those who do them but those who are interested in those who do them. I wish people will run away from these acts and turn their lives over to Jesus, for they cannot stand the judgment of God.

b. **Incest**: Incest is defined at the dictionary.com as sexual intercourse between closely related persons. This is something that God does not approve of, but this horrible thing goes on in many homes around the world. The father cannot have sex with the daughter, neither can a mother have sex with the son, nor siblings, can have sex. Looking at Lev. 18: 6 "None of you shall approach to any that is near of kin to him, to uncover their nakedness: I am the Lord." Having sex with a close relative is an abominable before God. John the Baptist was killed just because he wanted to stop Herod from marrying Herodias, who was the wife of Philip the brother of Herod. Looking at Mark 6:17-28 "For Herod himself had sent forth and laid hold upon John, and bound him in prison for Herodias' sake his brother Philip's wife: for he had married her. For John had said unto Herod, It is not lawful for thee to have they brother's wife. Therefore Herodias had a quarrel against him, and would have killed him; but she could not: For Herod feared John knowing that he was a just man and a holy, and observed him, and when he heard him, he did many things, and heard him gladly. And when a convenient day was come, that Herod on his birthday made supper to his lords, high captains, and chief estate of Galilee; and when the daughter of the said Herodias came in, and danced, and pleased Herod and them that sat with him., the king said unto the damsel, Ask of me whatsoever thou wilt, and I will give thee. And he swear unto her, Whatsoever thou shalt ask of me, I will give thee, unto the half of my kingdom. And she went forth, and said unto her mother, What shall I ask? And she said, The head of John the Baptist. And she came in straightway with haste unto the king, and asked saying, I will that thou give me by and by in a charger the head of John the Baptist. And the king was exceeding sorry; yet for his oath's sake, and for their sakes which sat with him, he would not reject her. And immediately the king sent an executioner, and commanded his head to be brought: and he went and beheaded him in prison, And brought his head in a charger, and gave it to the damsel: and the damsel gave it to her mother: And his disciples heard of it, they came and took up his corpse, and laid it in a tomb." This is a sad incident, for John the Baptist was killed just because John wanted the king to do the right thing. Satan will take over your mind, if you are not a Christian, and will let you do anything that is abominable in the sight of God. I heard a story that I will like to share with my readers. There was a couple living in New York who had been barren for a long time. The mother of the wife came in for a visit and by the time this woman was aware the mother became pregnant. You know who was the father? It was the woman's husband. The husband had made the wife's mother pregnant. This is the world we are living in; morality at it worse. Another story, there was a man who has been living with the daughter as a man and wife. This man had been having sex with the daughter for over twenty years and they live together. Many people do not care about God therefore they are morally weak and will do anything contrary to godly principle and will never care to live right with God.

c. <u>**Rape**</u>: The definition of rape from dictionary.com is the unlawful compelling of a person through physical force or duress to have sexual intercourse. According to Rainn.org, 1 out of every 6 American women has been the victim of an attempted or completed rape in her lifetime (14.8% completed rape; 2.8% attempted rape). 17.7 million American women have been victims of attempted or completed rape. Looking at Deut 22:25-26 "But if a man find a betrothed damsel in the field and the man force her, and lie with her: then the man only that lay with her shall die. But unto the damsel thou shalt do nothing; there is in the damsel no sin worthy of death:" In the Old Testament times if a man rapped someone's wife or fiancée then that man is liable to death. It was a big sin to rape but nowadays rapping has become common all over the world. I believe rapping is one of the works of the enemy so as to get many people hook to his diabolical ways and finally get them to their doom. There are wicked men out there who are only planning to get young ladies and rape them. I think the ladies have to prepare themselves when they are going out. First they should dress smart, not exposing most of their precious private parts. If you expose most of your body like your stomach with the nipple out there, some foolish guys are going to be attracted and may come after you. Next get something like a pepper spray in your small bag pack which you can take out incase some foolish guy decides to attempt to rape you. Next do not take in too much alcoholic drinks when you are out. And finally when you are out there in the street, walk briskly like you know where you are going. Do not be afraid for those wicked people can easily know those who are new in their area. Parent talk to your children and let them know that rape is not a good thing. Let us talk about it and expose the wickedness of rape.

d. <u>**Adultery**</u>: The dictionary.com defines adultery as a voluntary sexual intercourse between a married person and someone other than his or her lawful spouse. Adultery is simply someone who is married but having an extra-marital affair. It is an eye soar and very common these days to see married people involve in extra marital affair. This also an act that is abomination before God. There may be a problem in the marriage but it does not give any partner the right to get involve in extra marital affair. Let say, when the marriage got started, everything was good including sex, but as the man grew older his desire for sex had been don e away or he was faced with a erectile dysfunction, and as such could do nothing in bed. The couple should sit down and discuss for there is a lot of medication out there that will be able to bring back the sexual desires. There is no need for the woman to seek solace some where. Let us look at Mat. 19:3-9 "The Pharisees also came to him, and saying unto him, Is it lawful for a man to put away his wife for every cause? And he answered and said unto them, Have ye not read, that he which made them made them male and female, and he said for this cause shall a man leave father and mother, and shall cleave to his wife: and the twain shall be one flesh. What therefore what God hath joined together, let not man put asunder. They say unto him, Why did Moses then command to give a written of divorcement, and to put her away? He said unto them, Moses because of the hardness of your hearts suffered you to put away your wives: but from the beginning it was not so. And I say unto you, Whosoever shall put away his wife, except it be for fornication, and shall marry another, committeth adultery: and whoso marrieth her which is put away doth commit adultery. Adultery is connect to marriage so when the Pharisees came to Jesus with the intention of getting Jesus trap in an akward situation, they asked Jesus if a man could divorce the wife for any apparent reason? Jesus told them no the only exception is when there is fornication involve. If you divorce, then you are not suppose to get marry for if you do you have committed adultery. If someone marry anyone who has been divorce the person also commit adultery. Let us look at Rom. 7: 2-3 "For the woman which hath an husband is bound by law to her husband so long as he liveth; but if the husband be dead, she is loosed from the law of her husband. So then if, while her husband liveth, she be married to another man, she shall be called an adulteress: but if her husband be dead, she is free from that law; so that she is no adulteress, though she be married to another man. According to the Word of God the only thing that can separate marriage is death. If a partner dies then the living partner can get married. Jesus did not allow the Pharisees to intimidate him to water down God's plan about marriage. In the same way John the Baptist was bold to confront Herod the king even at the point of death. Nowadays, preachers just want big congregation therefore, they have compromise the Word of God. It is time we get preachers like John the Baptist who was able to stand for the truth even at the point of death. Simply put God is against divorce and adultery. Let us look at 1 Corinth. 6:9-10 "Know ye not that the unrighteous shall not inherit the kingdom of God.? Be not deceived: neither fornicators, nor idolaters, nor adulterers, nor effeminate, nor abuser of themselves, with mankind, Nor thieves, nor covetous, nor drunkards, nor revilers, nor exortioners, shall inherit the kingdom of God. The simply truth is that God does not take light of the following sins; idolaters, that is those who are worshipping idols, fornicators that is pre-marital sex, adulterer, that is extramarital affairs, and so many others, so those who get themselves involve either Christians or non Christians are not going to see the kingdom of God. Finally let us look at Heb. 13:4 "Marriage is honorable in all, and the bed undefiled: but whoremongers and adulterers God will judge." This means sex in marriage is the only thing recognize by God. God says He is going to judge adulterers. It is the Word of God that is going to judge us therefore, let us do our best to live according to the Word of God, so that at the second coming of Jesus you and me will be found as good servants who bear the fruits of the Spirit.

e. **Cohabitation** (shaking): This is when two people, a male and female are not married but are living together. They sleep in the same room share the same bed and have sex together. Many people live this life because they are not prepared to commit their lives into marriage. This way of living together is not approved by the Word of God. I believe with all my heart that it is not a good thing for a child of God to get him/herself involve in cohabitation. It is simply fornication, which is sex before marriage, or sexual immorality, which is a sin and cannot be condoned by the Word of God. There are people who are living this kind of life and even producing children and are still not committed to one another. Marriage involves commitment to your partner, children, and to yourself. We need to make money to take care of our family so we have to know how we spend the money that comes into the family. We have to pay the bills, rent, electric bills, home phone and cell bills, food, warm clothing for winter, and light clothing for summer. We need to take care of the family but in cohabitation one can neglect to take care of the other or will even leave the relationship. There is no commitment in cohabitation and it can be dissolved anytime without any hustle. It is an abomination to God.

f. **Prostitution:** Looking at the (NIV)Hosea 4:12 "My people consult a wooden idol, and a diviner's rod speaks to them. A spirit of prostitution leads them astray; they are unfaithful to their God." Consulting of wooden idol is common in Africa. The fetish shrines have wooden idol that can tell people who come for consultation, their troubles and how the troubles came about and how to solve them. These shrines use familiar spirits, which are spirits assigned to each person's family by the devil to give detail information about a person to the diviners or the shrine. Prostitution is a sin that should be done away from the life of a child of God. Prostitution is an act whereby a woman is using sex as a profession to make money. Money is the root of evil, and it does not matter, as far as Satan can get people to go against the Word of God, Satan will use money as a yardstick to hook people to any detectable thing.

g. **Bestiality:** The act of sexual intercourse between an animal and a human being. This is an abomination before God, but around the world, many people are in the habit of having sexual intercourse with animals, such a dog, cow, goat, sheep, and so on. Several diseases are going on that cannot be cure, just because the enemy deceive some people into having sex with animals. A friend of mine showed me a video in which a man was having sex with a dog. It was really scary and nasty, but the foolish man was enjoying himself. I could not finish watching it and I started crying. What kind of world are we living in? Looking at Lev. 20:15 "If a man lie with a beast, he shall surely be put to death: and ye shall slay the beast." God commanded the Israelites to kill any person that will have sex with an animal. The animal also should be killed. Both the person and the animal should face a firing squad. This act is an abomination before God. Satan is so crafty that he has been able to make the things that are sacrilegious to be the norm of the day, so everywhere in the world you would see people doing horrible things in the name of freedom and personal right. Let me tell you that what you are doing may be right to you but may not be right before God.

h. **Lust:** Lust is unhealthy for a child of God. It is a sin or a wrong to lust after a woman or something that do not belong to you. Looking at Matthew 5:28 "But I say unto you, That whosoever looketh on a woman to lust after her hath committed adultery with her already in his heart. Lust is usually a strong desire to have sex with someone especially an unknown person. Looking at someone's wife with a disdain eyes is lust and should not be encourage in our Christian life. The Bible shows us how to overcome lust. Looking at Galatians 5:16 "This I say then, Walk in the Spirit, and ye shall not fulfill the lust of the flesh." How do we walk in the Spirit? It is simply walking according to the word of God.

i. **Pornographic pictures or sexual films:** Some people have made it a habit of watching pornographic picture or sexual films for the purpose of excitement and arousing their sexual desires. It is not a good behavior for a Christian to watch pornographic picture and films. It is not the matter of the sexual films but others go to the extent of masturbating to feel good of themselves. This is an uncouth behavior that should not be tolerated by any Christian. Looking at 1 Corinthians 6: 12 "All things are lawful unto me, but all things are not expedient: all things are lawful for me, but I will not be brought under the power of any. I believe masturbation and pornography should not be entertained as it may lead from one sin to another. It will not be easy to get out of it if you allow the enemy to entice you in doing this ridiculous things.

Chapter Eight

Curses

i. **Curses:** What is a curse? It is a pronouncement or words said to invoke harm or injury, an evil thing or misfortune to come upon a person, group of people, a place, location, society, a house, city, state, or a country. Before I get into the type of curses, I want you to know that Jesus Christ has done away with any curse, which, was against humanity. A person only has to believe what Jesus has done and accept Jesus Christ as his/her Savior and Lord for all curses on such a person to be broken. Looking at Gal 3:13-14 "Christ hath redeemed us from the curse of the law, being made a curse for us: for it is written, Curse is every one that hangeth on a tree: That the blessing of Abraham might come on the Gentiles through Jesus Christ; that we might receive the promise of the Spirit through faith." The point is humanity is not, only redeemed from the curses of the law but the blessings of Abraham, the father of all faith, have been pronounced upon us. Abraham was the riches and wealthiest person of his time, he was like today's Bill Gate. This is the kind of blessings, which God has invoked on all those, who will believe in what His Son, Jesus Christ has done for humankind. Let us look at Genesis to check on the blessings of Abraham; Looking at Gen 12:1-3 "Now the Lord had said unto Abram, Get thee out of thy country, and from thy kindered, and from thy father's house, unto a land that I will shew thee: And I will make of thee a great nation, and I will bless thee, and make thy name great; and thou shalt be a blessing: And I will bless them that bless thee, and curse him that curseth thee: and in thee shall all the families of the earth be blessed." Like curses are invoked or pronounced, in the same way blessings are also invoked or pronounced. God pronounced his blessings on Abram with only one condition which needed to be fulfilled for the blessing to come to pass. Abram was to leave from his father's house, and country and to travel to an unknown country. Abram trusted God and did what God asked him to do. Abram received the blessings; his name became great and we cannot talk about Jesus without his great, great, descendant, Abraham. I like the blessing of Abraham, for anyone who blesses me is bless but anyone who dares to curse me is cursed. This is amazing for God has pronounced this blessings, for all the descendants of Abraham, today's Christians included. Let us look at Gen 17: 1-8 "And when Abram was ninety years old and nine, the Lord appeared to Abram, and said unto him, I am the Almighty God; walk before me, and be thou perfect. And I will make my covenant between me and thee, and will multiply thee exceedingly. And Abram fell on his face: and God talked with him, saying, As for me, behold, my covenant is with thee, and thou shalt be a father of many nations. Neither shall thy name any more be called Abram, but thy name shall be Abraham; for a father of many nations have I made thee. God did what He said unto Abraham, for God bless him, made him father of many nations, and made a covenant with him. God changed Abram (childless father) name to Abraham (father of many nations). In the same way God has made a covenant with every Christian and He will change our names from fathers of poverty to fathers of riches, as we abide by His Word. Now let us look at the curses that Satan and his wicked forces can entangle people with and to put them in bondage.

a) **Hereditary curses**: These are curses, which are transfer from parents to children and children's children. A family can be curse with premature death and this will be a recurrence in the family until this curse is broken. Looking at Num. 14:18 "The Lord is longsuffering, and of great mercy, forgiving iniquity and transgression, and by no means clearing the guilty, visiting the iniquity of the fathers upon the children unto the third and fourth generation." From this verse, it is concluded that God himself is going to see that the sins or the wrongdoing of the fathers are going to follow the family even to the third and fourth generation. If a generation is twenty years then for between 60years to 80years, the children born into the family are going to be, affected by the wrong doings or the sins of their fathers. I am fifty-seven years old and I have never seen anyone from my family either from my father or mother side being successful in life. My father died in his poverty and all my four uncles who are dead, all died in their poverty. I became a Christian and decided to break the curse of poverty over my family. It has not been easy but I have seen some improvement as many of my family members have become Christians. I was the only university graduate but the family can now boast of five graduates and many more are in the pipeline. This hereditary curse was broken during the time of Ezekiel when the prophet of God said the following in Ezek. 18:2-4 "What mean ye, that ye use this proverb concerning the land of Israel, saying, the fathers have eaten sour grapes, and the children's teeth are set on edge? As I live, saith the Lord God, ye shall not have occasion any more to use this proverb in Israel, Behold all souls are mine; as the soul of the father, so also the soul of the son is mine:

the soul that sinneth it shall die." From these verses it can be seen that sin and curses are interconnected. I want you to know that the hereditary curse has been done away. Everyone individual action can bring a curse on him/her. Curse is not an easy thing to play with. I have seen a family who are never successful in marriage. The men will get married and divorce so easily for no apparent reason and their women likewise will never get a good married. Let me give you an example, my father married and divorced seven good times before he died. That is a cures and if his children do not take care they are going to follow the same suite. Thanks be to God, almost all of his children are now Christians, with few unbelievers so the curse of divorce is broken and we will be able to maintain our marriages. I know a man that was a thief, a real burglar and all his children followed his footsteps, and many of his children were imprison. A person may take some huge sum of money form one person for some kind of service which will never be provided, and the victim may be offended and may curse this person. This curse may follow the person and his children and children's children until somewhere along the line one of them get to know the Lord for this curse to be broken. Some of the curses that can be hereditary are; poverty, sickness, divorce, untimely death, and never getting breakthrough in life. Note what you do with your life will not only affect you but your children and children's children therefore it is better to live a life dedicated to God. God has given us our will, but any choice that we make in life, has it consequence and we should be prepared to accept the result. I know a friend who was a womanizer; he impregnated and had six children with six different women before he became a Christian. He is now married but he regretted living such a life.

b) **<u>Curses of the ground</u> (earth):** Looking at Gen. 3:17-18 "And unto Adam he said, Because thou hast hearkened unto the voice of thy wife, and hast eaten of the tree, of which I commanded thee saying, Thou shalt not eat of it: curse is the ground for thy sake: in sorrow shalt thou eat of it all the days of your life; Thorns also and thistles shall it bring forth to thee; and thou shalt eat the herb of the field." The fall of man in the garden of Eden come along with the curse of the earth or ground. In Ghana, the fetish priests and diviners can protect anyone with their black powers using the curse of the ground. They will prepare a talisman give to the person who is seeking protection from them to hide the talisman under their bed or hide it in the ground at the door post, just before the person enter his/her room. The power in this talisman is able to work to protect the person, until the talisman, is uncovered, by another person. In Ghana or most African countries, someone can invoke the curse of the ground on another person by either pouring a libation with an alcoholic drink or using a stream or a river to invoke the incantation on another person. I narrated in my first book entitled, "Effective Prayers" how a friend of mine died because a lady he got pregnant and deny invoked the curse of Antoa Nyama (a small river in Asante Region in Ghana) on this good friend. After three days his stomach got swollen and he was sent to the hospital but nothing could be done to save him. He died miserably to show that he was the one who impregnate the lady. If you offend someone then Antoa Nyama will vindicate the person just by killing you. Many Christians can do anything they want and go scot-free not with the idol worshippers. They are afraid of their shrines so they will do their best not to cause harm to anyone. Our God will not kill you just by sinning or offending someone but I wish Christians will live in reverence to our God who forgives and always give us the chance to live right with Him. The ground was curse with thorns and the Jews knew thorns to be curse that was why they plat a crown of thorns and put it on the head of Jesus, meaning to them, Jesus was a king of curses, and in so doing Jesus took away the curse of the earth. Looking at Matthew 27:29 "And when they had platted a crown of thorns, they put it upon his head," They knew that the thorn was a symbol of curse and they did not want to accept that Jesus was the king of the Jews so they decided to make him king of curses and that was why they put a crown of thorns on his head. Jesus Christ is unspeakable gift, a gift from our Father, the Almighty God.

c) **Curses of the air** (atmosphere): The curse of the earth also affected the air around the earth, or the atmosphere. That is why the Bible says anyone hang on a tree is a curse; this is because the heaven has rejected such a person and the earth or the people have also rejected such a person. Looking at Deut 21:22-23 "And if a man have committed a sin worthy of death, and he be to be put to death, and thou hang him on the tree: His body shall not remain all night upon the tree, but thou shalt in any wise bury him that day; (for he that is hanged is accursed of God;) that thy land be not defiled, which the Lord thy God giveth thee for an inheritance." In Ghana and most African countries, the curse of the atmosphere, or the air is used by the diviners and fetish priests, to develop protection talisman which is hang at the door post or on the neck of the person seeking the protection. Such a talisman should not touch the ground, for as soon as it touches the ground it loses its power. This talisman can also be wear at the waist. The funny thing is these protective talismans can lose their power, as soon as they touch the ground, why should people go to the fetish priests to pay huge sum of money for such a protection? Let look at sicknesses, for there are water borne diseases (which is the curse of the earth, or ground) and air borne diseases (which is the curse of the air).

Christians are protected from all this kind of diseases, and even if we fall sick we should know that by the stripes of Jesus Christ, we are healed.

d) **Curses from your own words**: Our words are powerful. Our words can make a way for us or can destroy our future. Looking at Prov.18:20-21 "A man's belly shall be satisfied with the fruit of his mouth; and with the increase of his lips shall he be filled. Death and life are in the power of the tongue: and they that love it shall eat the fruit thereof." There is power in our mouth or tongue therefore, we have to be mindful of what we say. If you say to your husband or wife, "I have regretted marrying you", then your marriage is heading for divorce for there is power in what you have said. If you say to your child "you are a good for nothing child, you are a thief and you will end up in prison," you have said it and you child is going to end up in prison. What you said concerning your life will surely come to pass for there is power in your tongue. Your own words can be poison or a curse for your life and your own words can be a blessing and life for you. Looking at Prov. 23:7 "For as he thinketh in his heart, so is he:" I started thinking of writing Christian books, always praying about the books and by God's grace my first book entitled "Effective Prayers was published. This is my second book but I am still thinking of a third book before I will relax. Think good of yourself and say good things to your life. Do not allow the situation in which you find yourself dictates you life, for we walk by faith and not by sight. The Bible says wealth and riches will be in your house, then, start living as if you are rich and pray constantly trust in God and He will let you know what to do to get rich. If you say, life is difficult for you and you cannot make it, then life is going to be difficult for you because that is what you are predicting for your own life. Be careful what you say and what you believe.

e) **Curses from your choices**: You may not know but your choice can bring curse into your life and at the same time, your choice may bring blessings into your life. Looking at Deut 30:19-20 "I call heaven and earth to record this day against you, that I have set before you life and death, blessing and cursing: therefore choose life, that both thou and thy seed may live: That thou mayest love the Lord thy God, and that that mayest obey his voice, and that mayest cleave unto him: for he is thy life, and the length of thy days: that thou mayest dwell in the land which the Lord sware unto thy fathers, to Abraham, to Isaac, and to Jacob, to give them." These verses show that there is a choice to be made in our everyday decision making. We can choose life and blessing or death and cursing. I want you to know that, you are who you are, because of the choices you made yesterday. Every choice we make affect our present and the future. If we choose to love God, obey his word and live according to his word and cleave or walk with him, then we are going to be blessed. But if we choose to live life our own way without knowing God and live as we wish then we should be prepared to face any life consequences that will come our way. You can be a child of God, but your wrong choices can end you to be under a curse. For instance, God may be calling me to be a minister of his word, or to be a missionary but because I have a very lucrative job, I will never listen to the voice of God. My job then is more important to me than to do the work of God. I may be going my own way and I may miss the blessing that God has bestowed along the line for me. I may be hit with termination from my lucrative job and there may be a lot of problems in the house which may end up with divorce and a broken home. It is better to listen to the voice of God rather than to listen to that of a man. This world is full of trouble but those with the Lord are not alone when they are getting through a tough time. The Lord Jesus will be with them but if you are not a Christian then you have to face these worldly problems on your own. This may be weary depressed and tiresome. Choices that we make daily are very important for they are going to affect us and if we are married then the children and the whole family. Rejecting God in one's life is the most unfortunate decision a person can make and choosing God is the best decision ever.

f) **Curses from someone's words**: A person can adjure a curse on another person if especially there is a grudge or some misunderstanding or something, which needs to be settled. A friend of mine got a lady pregnant and denied it. The girl did not waste time but curse my friend with Antoah Nyama (a small stream in the Ashanti Region in Ghana) and within one week, the stomach of my friend got swollen until he died. My friend made a very bad choice and died. Looking at Josh. 6:26 "And Joshua adjure them at that time, saying, Cursed be the man before the Lord, that riseth up and buildeth this city Jericho: he shall lay the foundation thereof in his firstborn, and in his youngest son shall he set up the gates of it." Joshua was a man of God so there was power in his tongue, and Joshua knew that. If anyone would be so foolish to build Jericho, then the person was going to lay the foundation with the death of his first born and set up the gate with the death of his lastborn. Someone who was stupid rose up to build Jericho and the firstborn died as the person lay the foundation and the last born died as the gates of Jericho were set up. Looking at 1King. 16:34 "In his (*king Ahab*) days did Hiel the Bethelite build Jericho: he laid the foundation thereof in Abiram, his firstborn, and set up the gates thereof in his youngest son Segub, according to the word of the Lord, which he spake by Joshua the son of Nun." Hiel was a stubborn person who thought nothing would happen. He built Jericho at the cost of his two children. When a curse is pronounced we should not take it light for Satan and his forces are out there working hard to bring the curse to pass. As Christians, we should know that there is power in whatever we say, especially, if we are grounded in the Word of God and our faith in the Word is not shaken.

g) **Curses upon a geographic area**: There are areas or locations, which the enemy has taken as his domain where wickedness only prevail in such area. The location or the area is supposed to be under a curse. Such an area, may be infected with drugs, drug dealers, guns and violence. Most of the people living in these areas do not value human life and can hunt and kill a person like hunting a deer. Looking at Psalm 9:17 "The wicked shall be turned into hell, and all the nations that forget God." This means the wicked is curse and would not prosper and all the nation that forget God, would also be cursed. Africa was known as the dark continent, this was because the people living on the whole wide continent at that time do not know God and were pagans, uncivilized and barbaric. I can say that Africa is no more a dark continent, for many people in Africa have known the Lord Jesus, especially in Ghana, I am not afraid to say that about 60% Ghanaians are now Christians. Many Christians in Ghana are praying and I believe Ghana is going to be like a beacon of Africa. Pastors, have to be aware of the forces of darkness operating in the area where they minister in order to pray against the works of the enemy and any curses impose on the area. For instance in Africa, a whole village will be under a curse, the wizards, witches, fetish priests, traditional herbalists, the spirits of the forest and the rivers, will be operating together to bring the village under Satanic influence. If one becomes a Christian in such a village then, such a person needs continues prayers and walking in the Word of God to overcome the forces of darkness that will come against him/her. When I became a Christian, there were lots of things going on in my family. My great grand fathers were idol worshippers, this brought the curse of untimely death, therefore, the men in the family could not grow pass the age of fifty and they would died. The next thing to worry about was poverty. It was like a disease in the family, for everyone was poor. It took time for me to know what to do about my situation but thank God I studied the Word of God and I was able to know what to do. I prayed and fasted to break the spirit of untimely death hovering around the men in my family and my prayers were answered. I am now fifty-eight years, and my senior brother is sixty-two and I have an uncle who is sixty-one. We have all passed the fifty-year mark. Our God is good. The family is still poor but I believe God is in the process of time will get us out of poverty.

h) **Curses of sickness and diseases**: Most people who are cursed come up with incurable diseases. I have seen three people who were curse with Atoa Nyama in Ghana and all of them came up with incurable diseases and died in a week's time. Looking at Deut.7:15 "And the Lord will take away from thee all sickness, and will put none of the evil diseases of Egypt, which thou knowest, upon thee; but will lay them upon all them that hate thee." So if we are going to live according to the Word of God and believe that we are going to be sickness free, then it will be so for us. Even when we get sick, God is going to take care of that. Why is it that God is going to take good care of us? The answer can be found in Deut 7:6 "For thou are a holy people unto the Lord thy God: the Lord thy God hath chosen thee to be a special people unto himself, above all people that are upon the face of the earth." We are special people for we are the elects of God, therefore God take special care about our lives. All that God wants us to do is to believe in His Word and live a life worthy of the vocation of our calling. Looking at 1Peter 2:9 "But ye are a chosen generation, a royal priesthood, an holy nation, a peculiar people; that ye should shew forth the praises of him who hath called you out of darkness into his marvelous light." We a chosen generation, the election of God therefore God will not allow any evil disease or any incurable sickness to come unto us. Our God is faithful, and He will watch over every Word of His to perform it. The devil will do anything to put many Christians in disbelieve and bring in deadly diseases to such Christians. I want every child of God to believe that so far as you are living according to the Word of God, Satan can do nothing to you. Even if you died in Christ, you are going to be with the Lord. Let do our best to trust and rely on the Lord Jesus in every situation or affliction that may come our way. Let us look at King Asa, the king of Judah. He was a flip-flop person, in that, sometimes he would trust on God and do the right thing, and other times he would trust on himself or other people so in the end he died miserably. Looking at 2Chronicles 16: 7-9 "And at that time Hanani the seer came to Asa king of Judah, and said unto him, Because thou hast relied on the king of Syria, and not relied on the Lord thou God, therefore is the host of the king of Syria escaped out of thine hand. Were not the Ethiopians and the Lubims a huge host, with very many chariots and horsemen? Yet, because thou didst rely on the Lord, he delivered them into thine hand. For the eyes of the Lord run to and fro throughout the whole earth, to shew himself strong in the behalf of them whose heart is perfect toward him. Herein thou hast done foolishly: therefore from henceforth thou shalt have wars. When king Asa trusted on God, Asa was able to defeat the Ethiopians and Lubims who came against king Asa with chariots and horsemen, but when Baasha, king of Israel came against king Asa, Asa sought help from king of Syria. King Asa did not seek help from God so the seer Hanani told Asa that king Asa was going to be confronted with uncountable wars. Later on King Asa beame sick and did not seek help from God and because of that he died. When we do not seek help from God then we give the devil the opportunity to do any nasty thing to us. Looking at 2Chronicles 16: 12 "And Asa in the thirty and ninth year of his reign was diseased in his feet, until his disease was exceeding great: yet in his disease he sought not to the Lord, but to the physicians, And Asa slept with his fathers, and died in the one and fortieth year of his reign. From what Asa did, God does not appreciate it if we do not seek help from him. When we are sick before go to see a doctor, we have to talk to God or pray. Usually many Christians forget about God when they are sick. We have to pray for the touch of God, commit the doctor and nurses, who are going to take care of us into the hands of God. Pray for the right medication for the sickness and for God's healing. We have to commit the sickness and every situation that we may find ourselves to God before we seek a doctor's or any person's help.

i) <u>Deceiver, who does not honor God,</u> As Christians, we need to honor God with our spirits souls, bodies and our substances. We need to worship God in the Spirit. This means a total surrender of the inner person to God. Seeking God, daily with all your heart and not weekly. We need to be faithfully in everything that we do, especially, in tithes and offering to God. Looking at Malachi 1:14 "But cursed be the deceiver, which hath in his flock a male, and voweth, and sacrificeth unto the Lord a corrupt thing: for I am a great King, saith the Lord of hosts, and my name is dreadful among the heathen." The Israelites were not faithful to God, during this time, and God used the prophet Malachi to expose their deeds. During this time any sacrifice to the Lord should be a male sheep or lamb, one year old and without blemish or spot. A lamb which is lame, or blind in one eye could not be used. The Jewish people would always look into the flock and get a spot or lame sheep to offer as sacrifice to the Lord. The Jewish people were not faithful with their sacrifices to the Lord. In the same way many Christians are not faithful with their sacrifices to God, these days. Many Christians think all that the church is now looking for is money. Let me tell you without money we cannot do the work of God. The church cannot pay for mortgage or rent without money. The church cannot go into missions and evangelism without money. Children ministry, youth ministry, and the pastor's pay, cannot be accomplished without money. Simply, we cannot have a church without money. When it is time for tithes and offering, many Christians do not pay their tithes and some who are paying do not pay what they are supposed to pay, as tenth of their income. I have been to several places of worship and during offering the most common money is the dollar. Many people will be able to give an offering of five, ten, or twenty dollars but they will give one dollar and safe the money for ice cream, or some thing else after church. When you do such thing, you are not deceiving God but yourself. You are bringing a curse upon yourself for not giving to God what is due to Him. If you do that you are inviting the twin sisters; debt and poverty into your house. Let me tell you for God is concerned about what we give to the Church in term of our finances. Please start giving to God what is due Him and you will start seeing financial break-through in your life. Looking at Mark 12: 43-44 "And he called unto him his disciples, and saith unto them, Verily I say unto you, That this poor widow hath cast more in, than all they which have cast into the treasury: For all they did cast in of their abundance; she of her want did cast in all that she had, even all her living." If Jesus was concerned of people bring their offering to the treasury that time what about the present? When you are going to give your offering think of Jesus standing by your side and think of what he is going to say about your offering and tithes, then you will be able to give what is due of you to God. When you pay your tithes and offering right then you are inviting wealth and riches into your house, as Psalm 112:3 "wealth and riches shall be in his house: and his righteousness endureth for ever". As the children of God, we need to live according to the Word and the blessings of God will be our portion in the land of the living.

j) **Robbing God**: Another thing that can bring a curse on us is by robbing God. How do we rob God? If you do not pay your tithes or pay it correctly, and pay a handsome offering to the Lord, then you are robbing God. The Pastor and the church elders are accountable to the church finances and they are going to account to God how they manage the church finances. Just do your part and leave the rest to God. Looking at Mal. 3: 8-12" Will a man rob God? Yet ye have robbed me. But ye say, Wherein have we robbed thee? In tithes and offerings. Ye are cursed with a curse: *(that is a cursed square)* for ye have robbed me, even this whole nation. Bring ye all the tithes into the storehouse, that there may be meat in my house, and prove me now herewith, saith the Lord of hosts, if I will not open you the windows of heaven, and pour you out a blessing, that there shall not be room enough to receive it. And I will rebuke the devourer for your sake, and he shall not destroy the fruits of your ground: neither shall your vine cast her fruit before the time in the field, saith the Lord of hosts. And all nations shall called you blessed: for ye shall be a delightsome land, saith the Lord of hosts. My brothers and sisters in the Lord, if we do not pay our tithes or pay it correctly then we are invoking a curse on ourselves. Financial curse will come on us if we do not pay our tithes. What is tithes? It is one tenth of your income. For instance if you receive $320.40 per week, then your tithes for the week is $32.04. You pay your tithes before you think about your rent, feeding and any other bills. The tithes goes to the church. It is better for the church to come out with the finances of the church, the offering and tithes received the week before be announced in the church and any deductions for the members to know what is going on with the finances of the church. There should be good stewardship and accountability for the members to know what the money they pay into the church coffers is being used for. In this way many people will be willing to pay tithes and give happily. If we want to receive the blessings of Abraham then we need to pay tithes for Abraham paid tithes to the king of Salem, Melchizedek, after conquering Chedorlaomer, and saving Lot, Abraham brothers son, from the hands of Chedorlaomer. Looking at Gen.14:18-20 "And Melchizedek king of Salem brought forth bread and wine: and he was the priest of the most high God. And he blessed him, and said, Blessed be Abram of the most high God, possessor of heaven and earth: And blessed be the most high God, which hath delivered thine enemies into thy hand. And he gave him tithes of all." Abram paid tithes to Melchizedek, the priest of the most high God. Blessing started coming into the life of Abram after paying the tithes. Let us look at what happened after Abram paid the tithes: a) God confirmed His blessings in Genesis chapter 15, b) God made a covenant with Abram, c) God changed Abram's name to Abraham, d) Then Isaac was born in his old age. Abraham was blessed but untold blessings started coming into his life after paying the tithes to Melchizedek, the priest of the most high God. God through the death of Christ Jesus has made available the blessings of Abraham to us but want us also to pay tithes as Abraham did. We need to pay our tithes to our local assembly, so that the church finances will be good.

Schism: A formal division within, or separation from, a church or religious body over some doctrinal difference. There are so many things to bring schism in the church, for example doctrinal differences, rumor mongering, backbiting, in fighting, sexual immoralities, misappropriating of church funds and many others. Satan is so crafty and he knows what he is doing for his main mission is to dwindle the faith of Christians, so Satan will always find something to crack the unity that is in a church and in so doing come along with division. Satan is so crafty and will do anything to bring division in a church. Many denominations are now fighting whether to accept homosexuality or not. Many social issues can also creep into the church and when care is not taken these can bring a break up. In this modern time, things like rumor, backbiting, and misappropriating of church funds can cause schism in a church. In all things, the church needs to be careful to have a sound doctrine, established on the Word of God.

Diviners: One major work of the enemy is to work through people who will be able to contact the unknown through divination, so as to divert many people away from serving the true God. These people can be traditional healers in Africa, Voodoo priest in Haiti, Psychics, and many other diviners around the world. God warned the Jews when they were about to dwell in the Promised Land not to follow the doings of the people who were there. Looking at Deut 18:9-14 "When thou art come into the land which the Lord thy God giveth thee, thou shalt not learn to do after the abominations of those nations. There shall not be found among you any one that maketh his son or his daughter to pass through the fire, or that useth divination, or an observer of times, or an enchanter, or a witch, Or a charmer, or consulter with familiar spirits, or a wizard, or a necromancer. For all that do these things are abomination unto the Lord: and because of these abominations the Lord, thy God doth drive them out from before thee. Thou shalt be perfect with the Lord thy God. For these nations, which thou shalt posses, hearkened unto observers of times, and unto diviners: but as for thee, the Lord thy God hath not suffered thee so to do." The diviners can consult the familiar spirits and would be able to know a lot of things about a person who is coming to the diviner for consultation. The diviner will be able to tell the person his/her problems, and the cause of those problems, and how the diviner is going to tackle those problems. All these are the work of the devil for those coming in for consultation to believe in the diviner and to bring in more costumers or people who will be entrapped in the devil's cage of lies and deceit. Satan has given power to some of his agents who are people who are practicing witch craft and wizard. These witches and wizard can curse a person a house or a place and it will be done, unless such a person is a child of God. Satan has also given power to some of his agents to be necromancers, who are able to communicate with the dead. In Ghana and most African countries, if a person died and it is believe to be killed by a witch then the family may contact a necromancer to contact the dead person to know who killed him/her. These devilish acts are no more practice due to the widespread of Christianity, especially in Ghana. The fetish priests in Ghana are also diviners and can know the cause of a person's problem or sickness. Satan uses this means to enslave innocent people and cause these people to do his bidden. In Ghana and most African countries, many including well learner people, even those of high authorities like the president or members of parliament usually go and seek help from diviners. Looking at Hosea 4: 12 "My people ask counsel at their stocks, and their staff declareth unto them: for the spirit of whoredoms hath caused them to err, and they have gone a whoring from under their God." In the devilish realm, the staff is a symbol of authority, so innocent people go to the fetish and the staff of the fetish will be able to declare to them, why they are not prospering or they are unsuccessful in life. The fetish priest, will tell the consultants what to do in order to get out of their predicament. Satan is so cunning he will do everything possible to entice people, then he will use fear and intimidation to entrap and bond them to be his slaves and servants. Worshiping any deity, apart from the Living God is the work of the spirit of whoredoms (prostitution). This means there is a spirit, which is an evil spirit behind any work of the devil. Therefore there is a spirit of lust, spirit of enticement, spirit of rape, spirit of homosexuality, spirit of violence, spirit of hate, sprit of unemployment, spirit of fear, spirit of jealousy, spirit of misunderstanding, just to mention a few. The enemy can sent so many spirits to one person just to frustrate and depress the person. For instance, the enemy can send the spirit of unemployment to a person and no matter how high his/her education level, such a person will never secure a job. If the person is a married man and cannot take care of the home, then the enemy will send the spirit of divorce and if care is not taken, the family will be broken apart. If the person is a Christian and do not look for men and women of God who can pray and break the chain of evil spirits that are sent against him, he may find himself being homeless as the enemy send that spirit against him. When I got converted or accepted Jesus Christ as my personal Savior and Lord, in August 1984, God spoke to me saying, the enemy is going to use power struggle in the church, money and divorce to destroy many churches and ministries. As the years go by, I have seen many ministers who have divorced and remarried. Divorce and remarry is the order of the day in the church, and many ministers are being pushed aside due to power struggle in so many churches, and many different churches are spring up due to power struggle in many churches. Money which is the root of all evil is playing a major role in shaping many churches either for good or bad. The enemy is also using the spirit of misunderstanding to break friendships, marriages and to bring confusion in so many churches. There may be some misunderstanding between marriage couple, then, the enemy will see to it that he will send the spirit of confusion in the midst. The enemy will send the spirit of hate and abuse to this marriage, and if the couple do not seek prayers and godly counseling, then their marriage will be in a chaos and if care is not taken the enemy will come in with the last resort, the spirit of divorce. The enemy may send a spirit of rumor into a church and if care is not taken, there may be a split in the church. The enemy will not leave us alone as he sends his spirits to any Christian just to dwindle his/her faith in the Almighty God. The enemy may send the spirit of confusion, the spirit of frustration, the spirit of depression, and even the spirit of suicide to any person and if care is not taken, the person may end up dead. Looking at Psalm 118:17 "I shall not die, but live and declare the works of the Lord." As Christians, we are to live and declare the works of the Lord, so do not give in to death when the enemy attacks you with the spirit of death, when you have not even spend half of your God's given years on earth. In December 2014, I nearly died from Pneumonia and High Blood Pressure. I was at work and my co-workers had to call in an ambulance to send me to Jenniferville Hospital, where I spent four days in the hospital. In a week later after I was discharged, the enemy attacked me again and I had to spent seven days in Mercy Fitzgerald

Hospital, in Darby to be totally free from sickness. God will honor us with long life and prosperity no matter, what the devil will do. We only need to trust in the Lord. We have to pray for our children for the enemy is able to send the spirit of confusion and suicide to them easily, especially if they are being tease by their classmates or peers in school. Parents, we have a lot of work to do. It is not only making money by working three jobs to put food on the table for the kids and catering for their needs make us good parents. I do not do any job that will not give me the chance to help my kids with their school home work and teach them, especially Mathematics. As Christian parents, it is our first duty to let our kids to know the Lord Jesus and not the duty of the Children Sunday School Teacher. It is our second duty to pray for our kids, which I do almost every day. Looking at Lamentation 2:19 "Arise, cry in the night: in the beginning of the watches pour out thine heart like water before the face of the Lord: lift up thy hands towards him for the life of thy young children, that faint for hunger in the top of every street." We are to pray every night for our children, lifting our hands to God, to bless our kids, in school and everywhere, they will be and that, God will honor them with long life and prosperity, and also pray that at the right time God will bring someone who fear the Lord into their life as their marriage partners. We also need to work hard to take care of their physical needs. Then are we the parents that God wants us to be. The enemy is so cunning for he is doing his best to frustrate many Christians by telling them that their God cannot answer their prayers and God do not care about their situation. The systems of this world which is being controlled by the enemy is trying to make things harder and harder for everyone in this world, but we as Christians have a God who cares and no matter what be the situation, at the right time God may step into your situation and say to the enemy enough is enough. God will then restore to you all the years that the locust has eaten, for our sufficiency is of God.

Satan who is the enemy is so cunning and can transform himself into the angle of light. Looking at 2Corinthians 11: 14-15 "And no marvel; for Satan himself is transformed into an angel of light. Therefore it is no great thing if his ministers also be transformed as ministers of righteousness; whose end shall be according to their works." In Ghana some so called ministers, who majority are prophets will go to a fetish deity for black power and use in their ministration to the people, or their congregation. These ministers have disguised themselves, using the Bible in their ministration but the power behind them is the black power from the deity. Some of the prophets are good and really doing the work of God. I know a prophet who is a friend of mine, who God is using mightily to bless his children, including myself in the Philadelphia area. At first, I did not want to go to the services of this prophet, but my son, Isaac convinced me to go with him to see how God was using this man of God. I went to find for myself that he is really a man of God. How he applied the Word of God, and how he led the congregation into prayers was so amazing. Now anytime I am free, I will be the first person to the fellowship even before my son will come. I am now an adherent member of the fellowship. The ministry, which is Gethsemane ministries, is a fellowship of prayers. If you do not like prayers, then you cannot be a member of this ministry.

Another ploy of the enemy is to send the spirit of poverty and debt to anyone. Satan can destroy your business and hit you with poverty, and not only will you be poor but also, you will be in debt for you will borrow, knowing things are going to be well for you to pay back but you will never be able to do so as the enemy keep you in debt. You need a place like Gethsemane ministries to pray effectively with the men of God for Satan to lose his grip on you to be free from poverty. Pray and seek the direction for God to make you prosperous. God will lead you in the way which, you should go and God will also teach you to profit. I believe God is watching over his word to perform it, so if I wait on God He will show me the way I should go and He will also teach me to profit. The same thing applies to any child of God. God is prepared to bless us finically, so that we can financially support the work of God. Looking at 3 John 2 "Beloved, I wish above all things that thou mayest prosper and be in health, even as thy soul prospereth." God is calling us beloved. This shows how He loves us. God wish above all things that you will be financially sound and that it will be well with you. You health is so important to God so we should exercise to keep fit and eat the right diet to live healthy. We should also listen to him to know what to do to be prosperous or financially sound. If you do not know how to listen to God then get my first book entitled "Effective Prayers" at www.Amazon.com and you will not only know how to listen to God but know how to pray effectively for answered prayers.

Chapter Nine

The Works Of The Enemy

Covetousness: Satan is very tactful and skillful, he can let you covet something that does not belong to you that you may steal or go for it. Covetousness is simply being greedy for something that does not belong to you. If you are the financial director of the church, you may be in need of money so you may covet the church funds that you may steal from the church coffers. You may take some money and say I will put it back when I get it but you will never put it back. Satan is using poverty and covetousness together to get many people to steal and lie about their actions. Looking at Luke 13:15-21 "And one of the company said unto him, Master speak to my brother, that he divide the inheritance with me. And he said unto him, man who made me a judge or a divider over you? And he said unto them, take heed, and beware of covetousness: for a man's life consisteth not in the abundance of the things which he posseseth. And he spake a parable saying, the ground of a certain rich man brought forth plentifully: And he thought within himself, saying, what shall I do, because I have no room where to bestow my fruits? An he said, this will I do: I will pull down my barns, and build greater; and there will I bestow all my fruits and my goods. And I will say to my soul, soul thou hast much goods laid up for many years; take thine ease, eat, drink and be merry. But God said unto him, thou fool, this night thy soul shall be required of thee: then whose shall those things be, which thou hast provided? So is he that layeth up treasure for himself, and is not rich toward God." The man who came to Jesus did not make a mistake of asking Jesus to tell his brother to divide the inheritance for the man to get his share. Jesus knew the heart of this man. The man had not set his priority right, for his heart was for worldly goods, instead of the things of heaven. Jesus gave a parable for us to know that one's life does not depend on the riches, houses, wealth or the company that one owns but one's life is in God. God has given us a will to make decisions on our own but every decision comes with a consequence so we should be prepared for the outcome. What God want us to do is first to seek him and He will add the riches of this world to us. When we seek God first, then we will not trust in the riches but trust God to make any wise decision in this life. What is going on is many have forgotten about God and are amassing this worldly goods, which one cannot take along when one dies. If you forget about God then you are like the man in the parable and a time is coming when God will take your soul away from you then you are going to see how foolish you have been in this world. It is my prayer that every child of God will first seek the face of God to make even the little decision of our every day life. Let us live according to the Word of God and our live will never be the same and in due time we will reap what we have sown.

Wickedness: Some people are so wicked that it shows in their way of life. This person may have what a friend is asking for but he/she may say I do not have it. A wicked person is not prepared in any way to help anyone. Some people also turn out to be wicked due to some past experience, let say you help someone to secure a work at where you are working and this person turn out to be saying all sort of things to your supervisor just to get you fired, then if care is not taken you will not help any other person in your work place. Wickedness is a horrible thing that should not be entertained by any child of God, but whatever we do we should seek direction from God, even in the helping of others. I have a friend who was so kind that many people borrowed money from him and did not pay back, for they took his leniency to be his weakness. I told him to direct his affairs with discretion, and always sought the face of God before he gave a helping hand and it helped him a lot. Looking at Luke 16: 19-31 "There was a certain rich man, which was clothed in purple and fine linen, and fared sumptuously every day: And there was a certain beggar named Lazarus, which was laid at his gate, full of sores, and desiring to be fed with the crumbs which fell from the rich man's table: moreover the dogs came and licked his sores. And it came to pass, that the beggar died, and was carried by the angels into Abraham's bosom: the rich man also died, and was buried; And in hell he lift up his eyes, being in torments, and seeth Abraham afar off, and Lazarus in his bosom. And he cried and said, Father Abraham, have mercy on me, and send Lazarus, that he may dip the tip of his finger in water, and cool my tongue; for I am tormented in this flame. But Abraham said, Son, remember that thou in thy life time receivedst thy good things, and likewise Lazarus, evil things: but now he is comforted, and thou are tormented. And beside all this, between us and you there is a great gulf fixed: so that they which would pass from hence to you cannot; neither can they pass to us, that would come from thence. Then he said, I pray thee therefore, father, that thou wouldest send him to my father's house: For I have five brethren; that he may testify unto them, lest they also come into this place of torment. Abraham saith unto him, They have Moses and the prophets; let them hear them. And he said, Nay father Abraham; but if one went out unto them from the dead, they will repent. And he said unto him, if they hear not Moses and the prophets, neither will they be persuaded, though one rose from the dead."

Lazarus was the poor man who had sores all over the body. He may be filthy, dirty and smelly. He may be homeless, for he had been laying at the gate of the rich man. He may be depressed, rejected, lonely, friendliness, and penniless, but he knew God. If he did not know God, then he would not have been in Abraham's bosom after his death. Lazarus had a name, because he was a child of God. The children of God are so important and their names are written in the Book of Life. The rich man did not have a name because his riches was not important to God. One's social status, race or color is not important to God, if you do not have a personal relationship with God. This rich man was very wicked, for he saw Lazarus almost everyday at the gate, but did not bother to take a care of Lazarus. The rich man knew the name of Lazarus but Lazarus was not of his class, Lazarus was poor and he was rich. This rich man should have taken Lazarus into the house, dressed the wounds, put good clothes on Lazarus. The rich man should have done everything within his power to get Lazarus out of poverty. At least the rich man, should have taught Lazarus how to fish. The rich man did not have a relationship with God and his relationship with the fellow human being was also dead. The rich man should have been the good Samaritan for Lazarus. The rich man in hell, was being torment in hellfire and he lifted up his eyes and saw Lazarus in Abraham bosom. The rich man asked for mercy from Father Abraham but it was too late for there is no mercy after death. You need to work your own salvation with fear and trembling, while you live, for as soon as you die, there is no forgiveness of sin. You need to accept Jesus as your personal Savior and Lord while you are living or it will be too late when you die. The rich man who did not care about Lazarus in their time on earth, needed a drop of water from Lazarus' fingertip, but the rich man could not get it, because of the gulf that was between them. The rich man pleaded with Father Abraham to send Lazarus to his five brothers on earth to warn them so that they would not come to the place of torment. This could not be done, because the brothers had Moses and the prophets to hear the message if they want to repent. This modern day, the pastors evangelists, prophets, apostles, bishops, elders, of the local churches are the Moses and the prophets, we should hear them. As Christians, we should do away with wickedness and help one another to excel in our God given talents.

Thief: Looking at John 10: 10 "The thief cometh cometh not, but for to steal, and to kill, and to destroy: I am come that they might have life, and that they might have it more abundantly." Jesus describes Satan as a thief who primary aim is to steal; steal the joy of God's children and replaces it with sadness. When Satan steals any good thing, he will fill the vacuum with a very bad one. He will steal your riches and wealth and fill the vacuum with abject poverty and debt. He will steal your health and hand to you sickness and disease. Satan will assign his evil spirit to the children of God with the intention of getting them relinquish their faith in God.

The children of God need to be very watchful and pray daily to destroy the works of the enemy. Satan will not come only to steal but to kill. Satan will come in to kill your dreams, visions and destroy your ambitions and your future. Joseph dreamed a dream but Satan decided to fight very hard that Joseph would not be able to fulfill his dream. Satan will come in to destroy your home and kill your marriage. The couple that prays together stays together, for prayer is the weapon that we can use to battle the enemy and to destroy his works. Let me tell you, that Satan is not afraid when you are praying but not living according to the Word of God. We have to abide by the Word and our prayers cannot be hindered by Satan. Satan will covet something that belong to you and he will find a way to get it from you, if you are not walking worthy of your vocation of calling. Anytime he steals something from you he will replace it with an evil thing. Satan is pleased when he is able to infect a whole community with poverty, diseases, drugs, alcoholism, violence, guns and killings.

Slavery: The main objective of Satan and his forces is to destroy the human race and get as many as they can, to join them in their doom, which God has prepared for them, which is hell. Satan has so many strategies, which he is using to wage war against the human race. He used slavery in the time past and you will be shocked to know that there is still slavery going on in a different form. Many young women all over the world are being sold into sex prostitutions, which is a different form of slavery. During the slavery period there were tribal wars all over West Africa, and those conquered, and what we now termed as prisoners of war were sold into slavery, with the exchange of things such as sugar, guns, strong drinks etc., unimportant things were exchange for human beings which were transported from the cost of Africa to the America to work on the plantations. Many of the slaves died on the way to America and were dumped into the sea.

The Trans-Atlantic Slave Trade which rid Africa of its manpower was orchestrated by the devil to wipe out most of the able bodies black Africans from Africa. "The Trans-Atlantic Slave Trade began around the mid fifteen century when Portuguese interest in Africa moved away from the fabled deposit of gold to much more readily available commodity— Slaves. By the seventeenth century the trade was in full swing, reaching a peak towards the end of the eighteen century. It was a trade which was especially fruitful, since every stage of the journey could be profitable for the merchants — the infamous triangular trade."[21] It was fruitful trade for the Europeans but not for the Africans who, were being sold into slavery, and being transported into an unknown destination. If we start to look for money through any means fair or foul, the devil will show us to do any detectable things for the love of money. Looking at 1 Tim. 6:10 'For the love of money is the root of all evil: which while some coveted after, they have erred from the faith, and pierced themselves through with many sorrows." Money is very important in every facet of our living, but the love it will let people kill one another and will do anything to get it. The slave masters wanted to get rich and nothing else. The Europeans wanted to be rich and powerful so they did not care if slavery would cause any damage to Africa or not. Satan has so many strategies, which he uses for a period of time. He may modify his strategy and modernize it or bring it in a different form. Satan is very wise and crafty so we, as Christians should be aware of his tricks and devices.

Slavery was a means for the Europeans to enrich and to build the European empire. "Expanding European empire in the new found World lacked one major resource—a work force. In most cases the indigenous people had proved unreliable (most of them were dying from diseases brought from Europe), and the Europeans were unsuited to the climate and suffer under tropical diseases. African on the other hand, were excellent workers; they often had experience of agriculture and keeping of cattle, they were used to a tropical climate, resistant to tropical diseases, and they could be "worked very hard" on the plantations and mines.

During the eighteen century, when the slave trade accounted for the transport of a staggering 6 million Africans, British was the worst transgressor—responsible for almost 2.5 million. This is a fact often forgotten by those who regularly cite Britain's prime role in the abolition of the slave trade.[22] Britain played a major role in the abolition of the slave trade. "On February 24, 1791, just six days before his death, the veteran John Wesley wrote Wilberforce: "Unless the divine power has raised you up to be as Athanasius contra mundum, I see not how you can go through your glorious enterprise in opposing that execrable villainy, which is the scandal of religion, of England, and of human nature. Unless God has raised you up for this very thing, you will be worn out by the opposition of men and devils. But, if God be for you, who can be against you? Are all of them together stronger than God? O be not weary of well doing! Go on in the name of God and in the power of his might, till even American slavery (the vilest that ever saw the sun) shall vanish away before it."[23] By God's grace slave trade was abolish but the devil had used it to cause damages to Africa, which may take so many years to recuperate.

Annihilation of the European Jews by Hitler: Adolf Hitler was born on April 20, 1889 and died in April 30, 1945. He was born in Austria but migrated to Germany and became a political leader of the Nazi Party. During this time, Europe was experiencing economic and financial melt-down and looking for someone to blame. Hitler was able to put the blame on the International Jewish financier outside Europe, therefore, brooding the rise of anti-Semitism in Europe. Hitler was at the center of World War II in Europe and propagated the annihilation of the Jewish race in Europe. Hitler allowed himself to be use by Satan to get rid of all the Jews in Europe. Hitler saw the Jewish people as an enemy to the economic growth and prosperity of

Europe. During World War II from 1939 through 1945, Hitler and the Schutzstaffel (SS) with assistance from recruits and governments of the occupied countries, were responsible for the death of at least 11 million people in Europe, including almost 6 million Jews.

Killing of little children: Children are the future of every nation. They are going to grow to become the human-power of the nation. Some are going to be doctors, lawyers, entrepreneurs, even presidents and many others. Satan eyes are on the children of every nation and will do everything possible to kill, or get these kids into drugs, alcohol or anything that will be detrimental to their health and growth. When Jesus was born, Satan tried every means possible to kill Jesus and in so doing killed little children from a day old to two years old in and around Bethlehem to the coast. Looking at Matt. 2: 1-18 "Now when Jesus was born in Bethlehem of Judea in the days of Herod the king, behold, there came wise men from the east to Jerusalem, Saying, Where is he that is born King of the Jews? For we have seen his star in the east, and are come to worship him. When Herod the king had heard these things, he was troubled, and all Jerusalem with him. And when he had gathered all the chief priests and scribes of the people together, he demanded of them where Christ should be born. And they said unto him, In Bethlehem of Judea: for thus it is written by the prophet, And thou Bethlehem, in the land of Juda, art not the least among the princes of Juda: for out of thee shall come a Governor, that shall rule my people Israel. Then Herod; when he had privily called the wise men, enquired of them diligently what time the star appeared. And he sent them to Bethlehem, and said, Go and search diligently for the young child; and when ye have found him, bring me word again, that I may come and worship him also. When they had heard the king, they departed; and, lo, the star, which they saw in the east, went before them, till it came and stood over where the young child was. When they saw the star, they rejoiced with exceeding great joy. And when they were come into the house, they saw the young child with Mary his mother, and fell down, and worshipped him: and when they had opened their treasures, they presented unto him gifts; gold, and frankincense, and myrrh. And being warned of God in a dream that they should not returned to Herod, they departed into their own country another way. And when they were departed, behold, the angel of the Lord appeareth to Joseph in a dream, saying, Arise and take the young child and his mother, and flee into Egypt, and be thou there until I bring thee word: for Herod will seek the young child to destroy him. When he arose, he took the young child and his mother by night, and departed into Egypt: And was there until the death of Herod: that it might be fulfilled which was spoken of the Lord by the prophet, saying, Out of Egypt have I called my son. Then Herod, when he saw that he was mocked of the wise men, was exceeding wroth, and sent forth, and slew all the children that were in Bethlehem, and in all the coast thereof, according to the time which he diligently enquired of the wise men. Then was fulfilled that which was spoken by Jeremy the prophet, saying, In Rama was there a voice heard, lamentation, and weeping, and great mourning, Rachel weeping for her children, and wound not be comforted, because they are not." Satan is so pathetic for he does not care about the pain and anguish that will come on the parents who children are killed. When Jesus was born, the wise men came all the way to Jerusalem from the east. Looking at the time (which was almost two years) it took them to reach Jerusalem, they might had come from the far east, which may be around the land of Ur which was closed to the Persian Gulf. They saw the star, the star of the Messiah and they knew of the prophesy that "a Star will come out of Jacob" so they decided to come and look for the King of the Jews who was born. Christ came among the Jewish people but they did not recognize him when he was born, because the people were too much involved in politics of that time and were only thinking of the Roman occupation rather than the prophecies about the Messiah. The wise men who, were not Jewish but knew of this prophecy were all the time looking at the stars as they were shepherds and star gazers. Looking at the time that this prophesy about the Messiah was given by Balaam, who was hired by the king of the Moabites, Balaak to curse the Israelites when they were coming from Egypt to the promised land, to the time that the Messiah was born, was too long for the prophesy to be forgotten. Looking at Num 23:21 "He hath not beheld iniquity in Jacob, neither hath he seen perverseness in Israel: the Lord his God is with him, and the shout of a king is among them." This prophecy is marvelous, for Balaam was able to see the king shouting among the Israelites, and this is King Jesus. Balaam did not stop here but go further to give the outstanding prophecy which kept the wise men watching at the stars throughout their whole life to see the bright morning Star. Looking at Num. 24:17 "I shall see him, but not now: I shall behold him but not nigh: there shall come a Star out of Jacob, and a Sceptre shall rise out of Israel, and shall smite the corners of Moab, and destroy all the children of Sheth." Balaam was able to give a distinct prophecy of the Star that will come out of Jacob and this Star is Jesus. Balaam also said a Sceptre shall rise out of Israel. The Sceptre is a symbolic stick for kingship, which means Jesus the King shall rise out of Israel. These were profound prophecies but the people who these were meant for, missed the coming of the Messiah, but the wise men, who were looking forward to the coming the King of Israel did not. It took them two years looking and following the direction of the star to come to Jerusalem to look for this King. They were divinely directed but it was not easy to see and follow a star during the day so when they got to Israel, they used their human wisdom to think that a king would come from the city, so they went to Jerusalem. When Herod and all the people in Jerusalem heard about the new King that was born they were troubled. Why should they be disturbed about this new born King? This is because Herod though of his earthly kingship and was threatened by the new born King. Satan immediately used fear and intimidation to get Herod to kill all the children born a day to two years old, as the wise men went another way without coming to Herod.

Quite recently a sad thing happened in Sandy Hook as it happened in the days that Jesus was born. Sandy Hook has a population of about 11,000 and it is a small town in Newtown borough, Connecticut's Fairfield County. On December 4, 2012, this little town witness a mass killing of young children at Sandy Hook Elementary School, as a gun man killed 20 little children and six adults before killing himself. Satan is so wicked and will go out using any means to destroy the human population especially children.

Religious Differences: Religious difference is one of the tactics that the enemy is using to fight humanity. It is easy for people to get hook to their religious believe that they will be prepared to kill others who they may find threaten to their beliefs. According to CNN news on March 17, 2010, some Muslim herdsmen, some dressed in military uniform attacked, a predominantly Christian village at about 1:00 am on Wednesday near the city of Jos in Nigeria and about eleven people were dead. Recently, tension between Christians and Muslim in the Central African Republic has caused many dead. Canada condemns such violence against Christian and Muslim communities in Central African Republic. OTTAWA, Canada, December 5, 2013/African Press Organization (APO)— Following ongoing reports of violence in the Central African Republic, including a United Nations report today on an attack on civilians near the capital Bangui, Foreign Affairs Minister John Baird today issued the following statement: "Canada is very concerned by the recent acts of violence in the Central Africa Republic (CAR). We call for an immediate end to the violence against civilian populations of all faiths and on humanitarian workers active in the country. "Canada strongly condemns those fuelling tension between communities that have lived in peace with one another in the past. Freedom of religion is a basic right for everyone and is a priority of the Government of Canada. "We urge all parties in the CAR to refrain from all forms of violence, to facilitate free and unimpeded humanitarian access to those in need, and to respect the basic human rights of all communities in the country. "Central Africans deserve to live in peace without fear of persecution. We will continue to work closely with our international partners to follow the evolving security and humanitarian situation in the CAR. In 2013, Canada contributed more than $6.9 million in humanitarian assistance to help meet the urgent needs of those affected by this conflict." Africa is not the only continent where there is religious conflict. Religious tension can be seen in several places around the world. The enemy may cause tension between Buddah worshippers and Hindus, Christians and Muslim. Tension can erupt between any two religious factions in any place around the world. Satan's goal is to bring tension, which may lead to violence and killings so that Satan may be able to achieve his aim, which is killing and destroying the human population.

Terrorism: The main work of the devil is to bring terror, fear, trembling, and horror to humankind in order to cause disease, sickness, destruction and death to many or individual people. Looking at Psalm 55:3-5 "Because of the voice of the enemy, because of the oppression of the wicked: for they cast iniquity upon me, and in wrath they hate me. My heart is sore pained within me: and the terrors of death are fallen upon me. Fearfulness and trembling are upon me, and horror hath overwhelmed me." Terrorism is something that should not be condoned and connived by any person, group or government against any people. The devil is using the terror of death in bring untold hardship pain and death to many people around the world. Now, September, 11 is inscribed in the history of the United States of America, for the atrocity of terrorism lashed against this giant nation castrated by the unscrupulous person, Osama Bin Ladin. I could see the joy in the eyes of every American when President Obama was able to get rid of this son of the devil. America has enjoyed peace till this time, for the terrorist are now afraid that if they hit America, President Obama will come after them. I believe that is what Obama will do, so they dare not hit America again. President Obama has done a good job in keeping America safe. Now terrorism can be seen in almost every part of the world. It is the work of the enemy, only to get rid of as many people he could get in this end time. As Christians we should do our best to bring the message of Hope to every corner of the world, that is "Christ in you, the hope of glory". Christ Jesus is the only hope in this present time and in the time to come. If we are going to propagate the gospel, I believe many people will believe and be saved from the wrath of God that is yet to come on this earth. There are many problems that can be solved if the leaders are going to sit down around a table, that is use tale talk conference, but the enemy is using hate to desist these leaders to sit down. The minority side may then stick to terrorism to get their point across. I believe, we live in a civilized world so it will be better if we can find a better way of solving litigation, problems and difficult situations which arise between nations, and sometimes group of people in the same country, instead of using barbaric methods like terrorism.

Chapter Ten

Evil Spirits

Evil Spirits: Demons or evil spirits are common everywhere around the world. Satan is working hard with his evil spirits to bring killing and destruction around the world. There is one evil spirit known as familiar spirits, which Satan has dispatched to every single family in the world to know the activities of every single person in the world. In Africa, there are fetish shrines, where the priests are able to tell a visitor his/her name, the reason of visit and many other things using the familiar spirits. Looking at Lev 19:31 "Regard not them that have familiar spirits, neither seek after wizards, to be defiled by them: I am the Lord your God." Therefore Christians are warned not to go after anyone who uses familiar spirits for example the psychic, voodoo priests or any of the shrines in Africa or elsewhere. Our inspiration and direction in life comes from the Word of God and not from a psychic, or voodoo priest. Satan has dispatched the evil spirits only to go around and bring havoc to humankind. Some of the evil spirits out there are the spirit of divorce which comes in only to break marriages, especially Christian marriages and other spirits are, the spirit of poverty, spirit of unemployment, the spirit of drug addiction, the spirit of hate, the spirit of miscommunication, especially in marriage, to bring in confusion in order to bring chaos and divorce. There are so many evil spirits out there that I may not be able to mention. The spirit of pride, the spirit of greediness, the spirit of masturbation, the spirit of lust, the spirit of enticement, and evil eye, are all there and we as Christians should not allow ourselves to fall victim to any of these evil spirits.

There are evil spirits that have been able to possess a person and when a person is possessed then this person needs to be delivered before he/she will be free from the influence of the evil spirit. For instance, if the spirit of dumb possesses a person then the person is not able to talk, until the person is delivered. Looking at Luke 11:14-26 "And he was casting a devil, and it was dumb. And it came to pass, when the devil was gone out, the dumb spake; and the people wondered. But some of them said, He casteth out devils through Beelzebub the chief of the devils. And others, tempting him, sought of him a sign from heaven. But he, knowing their thoughts, said unto them, Every kingdom divided against itself is brought to desolation; and a house divided against a house falleth. If Satan also be divided against himself, how shall his kingdom stand? Because ye say that I cast out devils through Beelzebub. And if I by Beelzebub cast out devils, by whom do your sons cast them out? Therefore shall they be your judges. But if I with the finger of God cast out devils, no doubt the kingdom of God is come upon you. When a strong man armed keepeth his place, his goods are in peace: But when a stronger than he shall come upon him, and overcome him, he taketh from him all his armour wherein he trusted, and divideth his spoils. He that is not with me is against me: and he that gathereth not with me scattereth. When the unclean spirit is gone out of a man, he walketh through dry places, seeking rest; and finding none, he saith, I will return to my house whence I came out. And when he cometh, he findeth it swept and garnished. Then goeth he, and taketh to him seven other spirits more wicked than himself; and they enter in, and dwell there; and the last state of that man is worse than the first." When a person is possessed with an evil spirit, then such a person needs to be delivered from the evil spirit. As seen in Luke 11, Jesus delivered a person who was possessed with the spirit of dumb. If a person is delivered from an evil spirit then such a person should allow the Spirit of God to come and live within him/her. This can be done if the person accepts Jesus Christ as his/her savior. The evil spirit that was driven out will come and check if the place is vacant then the evil spirit will go and call many of his evil friends and they will come and inhabit the person and the person's state is going to be worse. The devil can send the spirit of premature death, poverty, sickness and disease to a person or a household. Let me give you an example; before I became a Christian; the men in my mother's side of the family never live past 60 years. When I become converted I started praying against untimely death in my family and God who answers prayer head me. Now there are two men in my family who have passed 60 years. Satan can send in the spirit of persecution, affliction, suppression, depression, and oppression to a person, a family, or an area.

War: War have been taking the lives of people all over the world. The devil will bring a little of misunderstanding between two nations, which may in the end, bring these two nations to fight against each other. Looking at Mathew 24:6-8 "And ye shall hear of wars and rumors of wars: see that ye be not troubled: for all these things must come to pass, but the end is not yet. For nation shall rise against nation, and kingdom against kingdom; and there shall be famines, and pestilences, and earthquakes in divers places." Wars are the norm of the day and within a tinkle of an eye, a war could spring up where no one expects. Quiet recently, there have been wars in Liberia, Sierra Leone, and between the Israel and the Palestine. A little misunderstanding that could be solved by a table talk-conference, would escalate into a war. War is the work of the devil, for The main work of Satan is to destroy humanity around the world. If Satan is able to bring war between nations, then he is able to achieve most of his diabolical plans and wishes.

The Spirit of hate: What is hate? It is a feeling or intense passion of dislike for a person, group of people or race, a place, or something. Most of the time something may trigger the hate in that person. For example I have a friend who hate going to Kessington area in Philadelphia due to the violence that goes on in that area. A black person may commit a heinous crime and because of that, someone may hate all black people. I want you to know that there is a spirit behind hate which, the enemy is using to destroy many marriages, friendships, homes, societies, and even churches. Looking at 1 John 3: 15 "Whosoever hateth his brother is a murderer: and ye know that no murderer hath eternal life abiding in him." You can not be a Christian and hate someone, for the color of his/her skin. There is no eternal life in anyone who hates another person. Eternal life is only in Jesus, so if someone accepts Jesus as a Savior and Lord, then such a person has eternal life, but may lose this eternal life if the person chooses to hate. It is a choice to hate or to love. There is a spirit behind love, which is from God, and there is a spirit behind hate which is from Satan. Looking at 2 Timothy 1:7 "For God hath not given us the spirit of fear; but of power, and of love, and of sound mind." If the spirit of fear is not from God then it is from the devil. Note there is a spirit behind fear and let me tell you, there is nothing that Satan will do without sending a demonic spirit to do it. As Christians, we need to reject the spirit of hate and fear but rather desire the spirit of love to reign in our hearts. We have to disregard any class discrimination and distinctions within our societies and nations. For instance in Ghana, most of the people from the Southern Ghana have no respect for the people from Northern Ghana, because the northerners come to do the menial jobs in the south that the southerners will not do. It will be difficult to see a southerner married to someone from the north. In Christ Jesus there are no upper and lower class people. We are all equal before the eyes of the Living God for God created everyone in His image. In many societies around the world, many people are look down upon because they are poor. The rich people look down on the poor people, and they would not like any inter marriages between the poor and the rich. The same go for the powerful and the commoner. Those in power will not allow any inter marriage between the powerful and the commoner. In such societies, because of class distinction, many people are not prepared to change the statue quo and thus will not accept Christianity, which teach that all men/women are create in the image of God, therefore we are all equal and precious in the eyes of God.

Lack of knowledge: There is power in knowledge especially if it is the right knowledge. The knowledge of the Word of God will set you free, therefore, Satan will make it hard for Christians to study the Word. If we study the Word then we will be able to know the promises of God for His children, so that Satan will not be able to destroy our lives. We will be able to know what God has promise us in His Word. We need to hold fast to the promises of the Word. The enemy will like us to lack knowledge so that we will not be able to know the purposes of God for our life. When you lack knowledge, you may die very young, cutting down your life span. In October, 2014, I felt seriously sick with my blood pressure at 215/117 and I thought I was going to die. I had shortness of breath and as if someone was trying to suffocate me to death. I could not speak but I remembered a verse from the Bible in Psalm 118:17 "I shall not die but live and declare the works of God. I started saying this over and over finally, I was able to call 911, an ambulance came and I was sent to the hospital. Looking at Hosea 4: 6 "My people are destroyed for lack of knowledge: because thou hast rejected knowledge, I will also reject thee and thou shalt be no priest to me: seeing thou hast forgotten the law of thy God, I will also forget thy children. The knowledge of the word of God is important for every child of God to lead life worthy of the vocation of your calling. Without the knowledge of the word we may live a life that may be contrary to the word of God. As Christians, we need to study the word of God and put into practice what we learn. We cannot be Christians and live life as we wish. If we do not study to know how God wants us to lead our life then we have rejected the knowledge of God and He will not only reject us but also our children.

Spirit of Laziness: The spirit of laziness is a tool, which the enemy uses to get many young people into poverty. If you are student and lazy, then you will never get your school work done. If you are a worker and you are lazy, it will show in the way you work, and you may be kick out of job. I think it is a decision to choose to work hard on anything that you are doing. Laziness is the pathway to poverty, so every child of God has to encourage him/herself to choose to work hard in this life. Looking at Proverb 6:6-11 "Go to the ant, thou sluggard; consider her ways, and be wise: Which has no guide, overseer, or ruler, Provideth her meat in the summer, and gathereth her food in the harvest. How long wilt thou sleep, O sluggard? When will thou arise out of sleep? Yet a little sleep a slumber, a little folding of the hands to sleep: So shall thy poverty come as one that travelleth, and thy want as an armed man." The ant is a small insect that has not much strength but it is a busy body always looking for food in the summer which, can be stored for the winter. God want us to be hard working as the ant, so that we will be able to save for the hard times. If we allow our beds to be soft and cozy for us then poverty will be knocking at our door. Looking at Proverb 22:29 "Seeth thou a man diligent in his business? He shall stand before kings; he shall not stand before mean men." If you are a hard worker, you will be recognized for your work, and it will be paid off and you are going to be in the company of the dignitaries. Let us choose to work hard for it will lead us into prosperity. If you are a man and you are lazy, then you will not be able to keep a family or your family will be shattered, for you will have no money to keep your family together. If you want to be able to put food on the table for your family, be able to pay the bills and go to the mall for shopping with your family then you need to work hard. Looking at Proverbs 13:22 "A good man leaveth an inheritance to his children's children: and the wealth of the just is laid up for the just." For one to leave an inheritance even for his/her children, one needs to work very hard, therefore, to be able to leave an inheritance for his/her children's children, which means, one needs to work extra hard. I will be pleased if I am able to leave an inheritance for my children and children's children, so I will work very hard to be a good father.

Spirit of pride: Pride and arrogance is something that, the enemy uses to get many Christians in losing their blessings. For instance, in Ghana, there are so many different tribes and some people from one tribe may look down on people from a different tribe. One time a lady that I know who is an Asante got married to a young man from the Ewe tribe. These people are Christians, and another lady from the Akuapim tribe said to me, she would never marry someone from the Ewe tribe. This lady is going to find it difficult getting a partner for in Christianity, there is neither Asante, nor Ewe for we one in Christ. Every Child of God has to do away with arrogance and pride to receive the best from God. Looking at Prov.16:18 "Pride goeth before destruction, and an haughty spirit before a fall." There is a fall, that goes pride, so to get a Christian to fall from faith in God, the enemy will bring the spirit of pride, and if the Child of God is not careful will allow pride to take control of him/her, which will finally bring a fall. You may not see if pride takes you up. Those around you may see it, but you may not get someone to tell you for most of the people around you may think they may hurt your feelings so they may shut up. Please if you are lucky to get someone to tell you then take it in good faith and pray against the spirit of pride to leave you. What is pride? It is esteeming yourself, better than others. We should not allow the enemy to entangle us with pride. You look down on others if you are proud, and you try to degrade and demean anyone around you. You see everyone as your servant and not your equal. May be you are rich and because of that you have no respect for the poor and the needy. They do not seem to work hard and they deserve to be poor. We have to respect every human being for we are all, created in the image of God.

The Spirit of Stagnation: The enemy will send this spirit to work in the life of an individual, a family a community or even a whole nation. I will define stagnation as a state or condition in which the flow or the running of a good thing in the life of an individual, a community or a nation ceases to flow. For instance, there can be an economic stagnation in a whole country, which means the economy has slow down and if the leaders do nothing about it, then inflation can hit the national economy or there can be an economic chaos. This economic stagnation will affect everyone in the nation due to the slow in the economy. Satan can send this spirit against an individual and if the spirit of Stagnation hits a Christian such a person will not see the flow of spiritual, physical, material and economic blessings in his/her life. The person may be working two or three jobs in order to make ends meet but may still be in debt. This spirit will see to it that one will not be able to make ends meet. The Spirit of Stagnation usually comes along with the spirit of debt and poverty. Such a person will never see financial blessing and will find it difficult to make ends meet, or even open a bank account. It does not matter how much more or harder, such a person works, he/she may not see any financial improvement in life. A person may be doing the same thing over, and over, again without any improvement in life, then the spirit of stagnation is working in the life of such a person. To overcome the spirit of stagnation, one needs to recognize the situation, and then pray about it. The next thing is to change your life style and start doing different things all together. Start paying your thites, if you are not paying it. Expect God to work a miracle in your life. Pray and believe God to set you free from the Spirit of Stagnation. Looking at 2 Kings 6: 1-7 "And the sons of the prophets said to Elisha, Behold now, the place where we dwell with thee is too strait for us. Let us go, we pray thee, unto Jordan, and take thence every man a beam, and let us make a place there, where we may dwell. And he answered, Go ye. And one said, Be content, I pray thee, and go with thy servants. And he answered, I will go. So he went with them. and when they came to Jordan, they cut down wood. But as one was felling a beam, the axe head fell into the water: and he cried, and said, Alas master! For it was borrowed. And the man of God said, Where fell it? And he shewed him the place. And he cut down a stick, and cast it in thither; and the iron did swim. Therefore he said, Take it up to thee. And he put out his hand, and took it." The sons of the prophets first recognized that where they were living was too small for them. They decided to do something about it. They would go and cut woods to come and enlarge their habitation. They would need an axe and none of them had an axe, so they borrowed an axe. When they were going to the bush to cut the woods, they invited the Elisha, the man of God to go with them. The man of God willing went with them and while they were cutting the woods, the axe fell off into Jordan and sunk. These sons of the prophets knew the principle of business. For example if one wants to start a business then, the person should be credit worthy to get a loan from the bank. The person can also do something to generate finds. For instance, the person can write a book or do something profitable to create wealth to start the business. The sons of the prophets, borrowed an axe, which in this time, may be a loan from the bank. They cut woods, which, they would use to build a bigger place for them to live in. The axe fell into Jordan and sunk. Which means they had lost the loan they got from the bank. They were in big trouble but thank God, they invited the man of God. God used Elisha to work a miracle, which, defy the principle of floatation. An axe head cannot float but it will sink. The miracle working God is able to defy the natural forces and cause an axe to float at the command of his servant Elisha. The sons of the prophets had Elisha, but the present day Christian has Jesus Christ, the Son of God, the Prince of Peace, the Name that is above every name in heaven, on earth or under the earth. We also have the Blood of Jesus Christ, which speaks better things than the blood of Abel, goats, sheep and cows; and this precious Blood speaks on our behalves. We have the Holy Spirit, who comes with the power of God to work on our behalves. We are more than able to get out of stagnation and command the blessing of God to flow in our life. Never lose hope if things are not working right, for at the opportune time God will intervene in your situation and bring you to your heights. We should not allow the enemy to use stagnation to hinder God's blessings for our life. We should recognize the situation in which we find ourselves, and do something about it. The most important thing is prayer. We may look for a man of God, for example a prophet, to pray with us, so that the mighty hand of God will lift any stagnation, which is encroaching our lives.

Let look at another example of stagnation working in the life of people from John 5:1-7 "After this there was a feast of the Jews; and Jesus went up to Jerusalem. Now there is at Jerusalem, by the sheep market a pool, which is called in the Hebrew tongue Bethesda, having five porches. In these lay a great multitude of impotent folk, of blind, halt, withered, waiting for the moving of the water. For an angel went down at a certain season into the pool, and troubled the water: whosoever then first after the troubling of the water stepped in was made whole of whatsoever disease he had. And a certain man was there, which had an infirmity thirty and eight years. When Jesus saw him lie, and knew that he had been, now a long time in that case, he saith unto him, wilt thou be made whole? The impotent man answered him, Sir, I have no man, when the water is troubled, to put me into the pool: but while I am coming, another steppeth down before me. Jesus saith unto him, Rise, take up thy bed and walk. And immediately the man was made whole, and took up his bed, and walked: and on the same day was the Sabbath. The Jews therefore saith unto him that was cure; it is the Sabbath day: it is not lawful for thee to carry thy bed. He answered them, He that made whole, the same saith unto me, Take up thy bed, and walk. Then asked they him, What man is that, which saith unto thee, Take up thy bed and walk. And he that was healed wist not who it was: for Jesus had conveyed himself away, a multitude being in that place. Afterward Jesus findeth him in the temple, and said unto him. Behold thou art made whole: sin no more, lest a worse thing come unto thee. The man departed and told the Jews, that it was Jesus which had made him whole. And therefore did the Jews persecute Jesus, and sought to slay him, because he had done these things on the Sabbath day." This story is so amazing, for this impotent man had been stagnant lying in one place for over thirty years. He had no one to help him, therefore, he was leading a very miserable life, of rejection, depression and loneliness. I love him for thirty eight years, he did not give up, but he allowed stagnation to take its toll in his life. When Jesus saw him, He knew this guy had been there for such a long time and he needed a divine intervention. Jesus asked him will you like to be healed? This is a simple yes or no answer but this man started giving excuses. Some sick people enjoy their pitiful state especially when other people start to pit them. This man wanted to be healed but he was full of excuses. Do not use your state as an excuse for you to sit idle without doing nothing about your situation. Do away with excuses and seek the face of God with prayers and sometimes fasting to come out in any situation in which you find yourself. This impotent man received his healing, because Jesus came by. The sad thing was that the Jews who were caught up with traditions and religion were seeking for a way to get rid of Jesus because He healed this man on a Sabbath day. How pathetic this was. A man who had been sick for nearly forty years been healed and the Sabbath day which is more important? Instead of rejoicing with the man, the sought to kill Jesus. I want you to understand that there are people in the Church who are like that. If God does a miracle for someone instead of rejoicing with the person, they become angry because, they have not received their miracle yet. We need to rejoice with those who are rejoicing in order to receive what we are seeking for from the Lord. Do not allow stagnation to slow or hinder your blessings.

Demonic Altars: Altars were built in the Old Testament time to make sacrifices to the God of Israel. Abraham built an alter when God asked him to sacrifice Isaac, the only son to Him, but after testing Abraham faith, God provided a lamb that was slaughter for the sacrifice. Altars were built and they were special places where the Jews could make sacrifices to the Living God. Satan and his evil demonic spirits also started building altars. Baal worshipers started building altars for the worshipping of Satan through Baal. That was why Elijah called for two altars to be built, one for the Baal prophets and another altar to be built for Elijah, the prophet of the Lord God of Israel. Let us look at the story at 1Kings 18:17-39 "And it come to pass, when Ahab saw Elijah, that Ahab said unto him, Art thou he that troubleth Israel? And he answered, I have not trouble Israel; but thou, and thou father's house, in that ye have forsaken the commandments of Lord, and thou hast followed Baalim. Now therefore send, and gather to me all Israel unto mount Carmel, and the prophets of Baal four hundred and fifty, and the prophets of the groves four hundred, which eat at Jezebel's table. So Ahab sent unto all the children of Israel, and gather the prophets together unto mount Carmel. And Elijah came unto all the people, and said, How long halt ye between two opinions? If the Lord be God, follow him: but if Baal, then follow him. And the people answered him not a word. Then said Elijah unto the people, I, even I even I only, remain a prophet of the Lord; but Baal prophet's are four hundred and fifty men. Let them therefore give us two bullocks; and let them choose one bullock for themselves, and cut it in pieces, and lay it on wood, and put no fire under, and I will dress the other bullock, and lay it on the wood and put no fire under.

And call ye the name of your gods, and I will call on the name of the Lord: and the God that answereth by fire, let him be God. And all the people answered and said, it is well spoken. And Elijah said unto the prophets of Baal, Choose you one bullock for yourselves, and dress it first; for ye are many; and called on your name of your gods, but put no fire under. And they took the bullock which was given them, and they dressed it, and called on the name of Baal from morning even unto noon, saying O Baal hear us. But there was on voice, nor any that answered. And they leaped upon the altar which was made. And it came to pass at noon, that Elijah mocked them, and said, cry aloud: for he is a god; either he is talking, or he is pursing, he is in a journey, or peradventure he sleepeth, and must be awaked. And they cried aloud, and cut themselves after their manner with knives and lancets, till the blood gushed out upon them. And it came to pass, when the midday was past, and they prophesied until the time of the offering of the evening sacrifice, that there was neither voice, nor any to answer, nor any that regarded. And Elijah said unto all the people, come near unto me. And all the people came near unto him. And he repaired the altar of the Lord that was broken down. And Elijah took twelve stones, according to the number of the tribes of the sons of Jacob, unto whom the word of the Lord came, saying, Israel shall be my name: And with the stones he built an altar in the name of the Lord: he made a trench about the altar, as great as would contain two measures of seed. And he put the wood in order, and cut the bullock in pieces and, laid him on the wood, and said, Fill four barrels with water, and pour it on the burnt sacrifice, and on the wood. And he said do it the second time. And they did it the second time. And he said, do it a third time. And they did it a third time. And the water ran round about the altar; and he filled the trench also with water. And it came to pass at the of the offering of the evening sacrifice, that Elijah the prophet came near, and said, Lord God of Abraham, Isaac, and of Israel, let it be known this day that thou art God in Israel, and that I am thy servant, and I have done all these things at thy word. Hear me, O Lord, hear me, that this people may know that thou art the Lord God, and that thou hast turned their heart back again. Then the fire of the Lord fell, and consumed the burnt sacrifice, and the wood and the stones and the dust, and lick up the water that was in the trench. And when all the people saw it they fell on their faces; and they said, The Lord, he is the God; the Lord, he is God." Elijah was accused by King Ahab as the one who troubled Israel. This was because Elijah commanded that there would be drought and no rain for the space of three years, and it was so. Elijah, the prophet threw a challenge for Ahab to bring the Baal prophet, to prove whether Baal was god or the God of Israel was God. The Baal prophets set up their demonic altar and prayed to their Baal but no fire came down. As soon as Elijah called upon the God of Israel, fire came up from heaven to lick up the altar. It was then before the Israelites saw the power of their God. The Israelites had been wavering between the worship of the God of Israel and the gods of the nations around them, so if the King was not living according to the statues of the God of Israel then the nation may go after the worshiping of other gods, therefore there were a lot of altars built for foreign gods and these alters were the demonic altars. Looking at 2 Chronicles 34:1-7 "Josiah was eight years old when he began to reign, and he reigned in Jerusalem one and thirty years. And he did that which was right in the sight of the Lord, and walked in the ways of David his father, and declined neither to the right hand, nor to the left. For in the eight year of his reign, while he was yet young, he began to seek after the God of David his father: and in the twelve year he began to purge Judah and Jerusalem from the high places and the grooves, and the carve images, he brake in pieces, and made dust of them, and strowed it upon the graves of them that had sacrificed unto them. And he burnt the bones of the priests upon their altars, and cleanse Judah and Jerusalem. And so did he in the cities of Manasseh, and Ephraim, and Simeon, even unto Naphtali, with their mattocks round about. And when he had broken down the altars and the grooves, and had beaten the graven images into powder, and cut down all the idols throughout all the land of Israel, he returned to Jerusalem." Josiah was eight years old when he became the King of Judah. I believe his mother Jedidah taught him in the ways of the God of Israel for the word of God says, teach a child the way he should go and when he is grown he would not depart from it. Josiah was one of the most remarkable kings of Judah. At the age of sixteen, he had reigned for eight years and he decided to seek after the God of David. At the age of twenty, when he had reigned for twelve years, he decided to break down all the demonic altars and grooves, which, were built for the worshipping of Baal and other foreign gods. Josiah was able to clean all the cities of idol worshipping and to lead the nation of Israel in the worship of the true Living God, the God of Israel. Christians have to deal with any demonic altars in their lives. This is because there so many demonic altars built around the world. Any shrine or place of worship that is not for the worship of true God, through His Son Jesus Christ is a demonic altar or shrine. There are such places of worship around the world. In Africa, all the fetish shrines are demonic altars. When a child is born, the parents, who may not be Christians, may send the child to a shrine for protection and well-being in life. When this child grows up to be a Christian then he has to break any affiliation with this demonic altar or the demons operation through that altar will continue to harass him. A family member who is not a Christian may seek protection for the family and your name may be mention without your knowledge, that is why you have to break ties with any demonic altars. When you become a Christian then, any affiliation with Satan or his demonic altars has to be broken or Satan can use the evil spirits associated with those altars to haunt you and you will never see any breakthrough in your life. I remember, When I was young, my elder sister who wanted to protected me from the witches and witchcrafts in our family sent me to a shrine where a lot of cut were made on my head and body and the priest put black power powder in these cuts in order to protect me from the witches. I was being protected by this demonic altar, so when I became converted, I prayed to break any relationship between this altar and me. I started to see breakthrough in my life, after breaking any ties with this demonic altar. If there is a know demonic altar in your life then pray to break any ties with this altar and you will see the hand of God working on your behalf.

Chapter Eleven

Satan Destroyer Of Destiny

Destroyer of Destiny: God has an ordained destiny for every child of His. Every child of God is to achieve great heights in every endeavor, but Satan will either hinder, or change the cause of action with the intention of destroying ones destiny or changing it for the worse. What is destiny? It is simply how a person's future or life is being shaped by unseen powers or forces. Destiny is the fate, or future state of a person that is predetermined or preordained by certain ordering of events which are caused by an unseen powers or agencies. Therefore, destiny has three parts, which are: a) It is the state of one's future, how the person is going to grow up to become. b) It is caused by preordained or predetermined events to bring about the future state of the person. c) This preordained events are caused by unseen powers. God knew you when you were in the womb. Looking at Psalm 139:13-16 "For thou hast possessed my reins: thou hast covered me in my mother's womb. I will praise thee; for I am fearfully and wonderfully made: marvelous are thy works; and that my soul knoweth right well. My substance was not hid from thee, when I was made in secret, and curiously wrought in the lowest parts of the earth. Thy eyes did see my substance, yet being unperfect; and in thy book all my members were written, which in continuance were fashioned, when as yet there was none of them." God has been taken care of you since when you were in your mother's womb. Every part of your body are written in the book of God, and an account is taken of every member of your body. Let say you have a disability, God knows and He will make a way for you to life a worthy life. God will take good care of you when you were born until the age of accountability, where you know what is wrong from right. Then you have to make the choice, either to worship God or deny Him or say, God does not exist. If one decides to worship God, then his/her destiny is control by his/her will and the Holy Spirit. For the Holy Spirit to fully, control the will of a person, then the person has to totally surrender the will to the Holy Spirit. God is prepared to let every child of His has a good destiny. Looking at Jer. 29:11 "For I know the thoughts that I think toward you, saith the Lord, thoughts of peace, and not of evil, to give you an expected end." God has good plans for your life. God plans to give you an expected end. That is from the womb God will take care of you, God will see you through this life and help you to reach your heights. Looking at Isaiah 58:14 "Then shalt thou delight thyself in the Lord; and I will cause to ride upon the high places of the earth, and feed thee with the heritage of Jacob thy father: for the mouth of the Lord hath spoken it." God is not only to see you through this life but will help you to reach your heights or will help you to ride upon your high places on this earth. You may pass through difficult times or be faced with so many hardships, your friends, and families may forget or reject you but the Lord will not forsake you. God will bring you out of the hardships and make you to ride on high places on earth. Looking at Habbak. 3:17-19 "Although the fig tree shall not blossom, neither shall fruit be in the vines; the labour of the olive shall fail and the fields shall yield no meat; the flock shall be cut off from the fold, and there shall be no herd in the stalls. Yet will I rejoice in the Lord, I will joy in the God of my salvation. The Lord is my strength, and he will make my feet like hinds' feet and will make me to walk upon mine high places." Habbakuk is saying that even though he has nothing to hold to and he is penniless he will rejoice in the Lord. Why? He believed, the Lord is going to make his feet like the deer and make him to reach his high place on the earth. God is prepared to see you through your life, even in your old age. Looking at Isaiah 46:4 "And even to your old age I am he; and even to hoar hairs will I carry you: I have made, and I will bear; even I will carry, and will deliver you." There is no doubt that if you yield your life to God, He will carry you through this life, He will give you peace and deliver you from any evil plans of the enemy. God's love, kindness and mercy will be your portion in this life. God has given us a will to choose so He will never force us to serve him. This act of worship should come from our own free will. When we worship and trust in the Lord, the Lord will be in covenant with us, love us, and all His promises are there for us to enjoy. Looking at Isaiah 58:10 "For the mountains shall depart, and the hills be removed; but my kindness shall not depart from thee, neither shall the covenant of my peace be removed, saith the Lord that hath mercy on thee." God will control your destiny and see to your well being in this life.

There are three things that control destiny, which are a) one's will b) The Holy Spirit, c) Satan and his forces. The destiny of a child of God is control by one's will and the Holy Spirit, while the destiny of any unbeliever is controlled by the will and Satanic forces. Let us look at how the will controls one's destiny.

Will: This is the power of consciousness, the ability of the mind to make decision, choices and act to carry them out. It is the power to dispose of a matter arbitrarily or being able to discern the cause of action. The will goes with discretion, which is the freedom or power to make one's own judgment and decisions and to act as one sees fit. Another word is volition, which is the act or faculty of willing exercise of the will, will power. We have to note that our actions are very important for what we do today will make us whom we are tomorrow. It takes years to build a name but it takes a second to destroy it. God did not intent to create us a robot so out of His infinite wisdom he created us with a will to choose what is right or wrong. Looking at Deut. 30:19-20 "I call heaven and earth to record this day against you, that I have set before you life and death, blessings and cursing: therefore choose life, that both thou and thou seed may live: That thou mayest love the Lord thy God. And thou mayest obey his voice, and that thou mayest cleave unto him: for he is thou life, and the length of thy days: that thou mayest dwell in the land which the Lord sware unto thy fathers, to Abraham, to Isaac, and to Jacob, to give them." God has given us a choice to choose. We should then be prepared to bear the consequences of our actions. How then can we make good choices? We need to surrender our will power to the Holy Spirit, study the Word of God and make choices or decisions in line with the Word. Let us look at Jabez, who was born in pain, so the mother gave him a name according to the pain she might had gone through. Usually, it is the father that named the child, therefore, for the mother to named Jabez, it means the father died before the child was born. The mother passed through pain and sorrows so she gave the name Jabez, which means I bore him in pain, agony and sorrows. Jabez knew that, that name was going to have a dramatic impact on his life, so he called on the God of Israel to change his destiny and God granted his request. Looking at 1 Chro. 4:9-10 "And Jabez was more honourable then his brethren: and his mother called his name Jabez, saying, because I bare him with sorrow. And Jabez called on the God of Israel, saying, Oh that thou wouldest bless me indeed, and enlarge my coast, and that thou hand might be with me, and that thou wouldest keep me from evil, that it may not grieve me! And God granted him that which he requested." Jabez was destiny to doom because the mother bare him in sorrows. Jabez did not accept his fate but called on the destiny changer, the Almighty God to change his fate, and God did as Jabez requested. Many people are suffering because they do not know the Almighty God. If you know the Lord Jesus as Savior and Lord, then you may need to pray to God, so that you will be able to attain your God given destiny. May be the enemy destroyed your destiny before you become a Christian, but as God granted the request of Jabez, God is still in the business of answering the prayers of His children, but you need to called upon Him.

Satanic Forces: Satan and his forces will destroy your destiny if you allow them. They will influence your thought process to make wrong choices and decisions. Looking at 2 Cor. 10:3-5 "For though we walk in the flesh, we do not war after the flesh: (For the weapons of our warfare are not carnal, but mighty through God to the pulling down of strong holds;) Casting down imagination, and every high thing that exalteth itself against the knowledge of God, and bringing into captivity every thought to the obedience of Christ;" Satan and his forces are wagging a battle against every child of God. Satan is making every effort to dwindle our faith in God and to get us to forsake God. Therefore, Satan is wagging a fierce war against us and the battle field is our mind. Although we walk in the flesh, the battle is a spiritual warfare. Therefore, anything that comes to mind, that is not in line with the Word of God, we need to cast it out. For example, you are looking for job and you have applied for jobs, and gone through all the processes. You have had the interview and you are waiting to be called to work. You know it is not easy when you are waiting, and the devil knows that. The devil will then bring thoughts into your mind, do you think you are going to be called for this job? This thought is not from God and you need to cast it out. Just believe that God will never fail you and He will get you a job. Let us look at another example; you are sick and had been prayed for by a man of God. You still feel the pains and tiredness in your body and the enemy would come in and ask, are you sure you are healed? Yes you just believe and trust God for His healing for the Word says by His stripes we are healed. Do not allow the enemy to tell you that you cannot achieve your God given destiny. You can, so fight the battle and trust God to give you the breakthrough. Satan will try to destroy your vision and kill your dreams, but do not give in to his diabolical plans. Do assess yourself and know what you are good in doing and make a plan and do your best to execute your goals. Looking at John 10:10 "The thief cometh not, but for to steal, and to kill, and to destroy: I am come that they might have life, and that they might have it more abundantly." The enemy will kill your plans or terminate any project or work that you set your hand on. The enemy will do his best to hinder you and will not allow you to achieve anything good. He will also hinder your progress and will see to it that you will not be able to reach you God given destiny. Looking at 1 Thess, 2:18 "Wherefore, we would have come unto you, even I Paul, once and again; but Satan hindered us. Paul wanted to visit the Thessalonians but he could not for he said "Satan hindered him". Satan can hinder any body with road blocks so that you will never be able to see progress in whatever you are doing. Satan can hinder your education, project, or anything your set your hand in doing. Satan will set so many road blocks in your life so that you will not be able to achieve your God given destiny. Child of God do not give up but with prayers and determination God will see you through. If you are not able to forgive what someone has done to you the enemy will be able to do away with your peace, and joy, and bring in depression, bitterness and pain in the heart any time you see that person prospering.

Holy Spirit: The Spirit of God will help us achieve our destiny in this life. God has given us a will so God will not force or do anything for us until we call upon him and hand over our will to God. Note that your strength cannot achieve anything for you. It is the Spirit of God, that is going to give you guidance and bring you to your heights. Looking at Zech. 4:6 "Then he answered and spake unto me, saying, This is the word of the Lord unto Zerubbabel, saying,

Not by might, nor by power, but by my spirit, saith the Lord of host." Zerubabbel was buiding the temple of God, in the face of opposition but God spoke through Zechariah the prophet that God's spirit would help Zerubabbel to complete the house of God. In the same way the oly Holy Spirit is to help us achieve our God given destiny in this world. God do not want any of His child to fail in this life. God is prepared to guide us and lead us the way we should go. Looking at Isaiah 48:17 "Thus saith the Lord, thy Redeemer, the Holy One of Israel; I am the Lord thy God which teacheth thee to profit, which leadeth thee by the way that thou shouldest go." God is prepared to teach us to profit, that is, God is going to tell us what to do, like the kind of business we should enter into so that we will be able to see profit in this business. God is also prepared to lead us the way that we should go. We are living in a fast world but God want us to slow down, so that we can get time for Him. God may be talking to us but we may not hear him for we do not have time for God. Looking at John 16:13 "Howbeit, when he, the Spirit of truth, is come, he will guide you into all truth: for he shall not speak of himself; but whatsoever he shall hear, that shall he speak: and he will shew you things to come." So as we bring our will in line with the will of the Holy Spirit, the Holy Spirit is going to guide us into all truth; the truth about your life, business, marriage, and destiny. God is able, so there is no need for us to run ahead of the Holy Spirit or behind it, for we will miss what God has in store for us. God is prepared to teach us what to do to bring success in our lives. God has given you a talent, that is unique and only you can bring this talent out to accomplish something big in this world. Looking at Joseph in the first book of the Bible, Joseph, was sold into slavery by his brothers and he was resold in Egypt but God had a plan for him. God had given Joseph a magnificent talent, whereby he was able to interpret dreams. He was sold into slavery because of his dreams but it was the interpretation of dreams, which got him out of prison. Two officers of Pharaoh were sent to prison where Joseph was an inmate. These two officers had dreams and Joseph gave them the interpretation. The butler was restored to his position to serve Pharaoh, but the baker was hanged as Joseph predicted. Joseph asked the butler to remember him but he forget about him for two good years until Pharoah had a dream and there was no one to bring an interpretation of Pharaoh's dream. The butler, then remember Joseph and he was brought in to give the interpretation of Pharaoh's dream and that earn Joseph the post of Agricultural and Finance minister in Egypt. Joseph was second to Pharaoh. Joseph was seventeen years when he had his first dream, which sent him into slavery but he was thirty years when he became a very important person in Egypt. It took him thirteen years of suffering before he had his breakthrough. Do not give up for your breakthrough is on the way.

I have already talked about Jabez, how he called on God to change his destiny and God granted him his request. What about Moses; when he was born every male child of the Israelites was destined to die, but Jocebed, his mother (where was the father?) was determined to change the destiny of her son, so she hid him for three good months. Jochebed had faith in the God of Israel so was able to change the destiny of her son. When she could no longer hid the little boy, she made a small ship for the baby and laid it in the river Nile, while the sister stood at a distance to watch what would happened to little Moses. Our God is marvelous and He will intervene when His child is facing a horrible situation. There was divine intervention, for Pharaoh's daughter came to the same spot to swim and she found this small boy in the small ship crying. She picked him up and Miriam, the sister asked if she could get a nurse for the child and her request was granted. Miriam brought in their mother and Jochebed nursed her own son and she was paid by the Pharaoh's daughter. To cut a long story short, Moses grew up to fulfill his God given destiny; that was to deliver the Israelites from Egypt, the house of bondage and to send them to the Promise Land. I love the women in the Bible for they were able to accomplish things that the men could not even venture to do. There were five women who were able to claim their inheritance among their father's brothers, when their father died on the way to the Promised Land. These were the daughters of Zelophehad and this amazing story is in Numbers 27:1-8 "Then came the daughters of Zelophehad, the son of Hepher, the son of Gilead, the son of Machir, the son of Manasseh, of the families of Manasseh the son of Joseph: and these are the names of his daughters; Mahlah, Noah, Hoglah, and Milcah, and Tirzah. And they stood before Moses, and before Eleazar the priest, and before the princes and all the congregation, by the door of the tabernacle of the congregation, saying, Our Father died in the wilderness, and he was not in the company of them that gathered themselves together against the Lord in the company of Korah; but died in his own sins, and had no sons. Why should the name of our father be done away from among his family, because he hath no son? Give unto us therefore a possession among the brethren of our father. And Moses brought their cause before the Lord. And the Lord spoke unto Moses saying, The daughters of Zelophad had spoken right: thou shalt surely give them a possession of their inheritance among their father's brethren; and thou shalt cause the inheritance of their father to pass unto them." These five beautiful, elegant and brave ladies were able to challenge the status quo for that time women had no saying in the affair of the family, community and state. Everything was decided by men who were leaders of the families, communities and states. If a man dies and has no son, then his inheritances are taken over by the immediate brothers. The inheritance were wealth, riches, land, wells (water) cattle, and many other possessions. The daughters of Zelophad were to loose their inheritance, as they had no brother to claim the inheritance for them. Being women, there were so many obstacles for them to clear before they could see Moses. They had to see their family head, that is the family of Manasseh, and the community head, and to the priest before they could come to Moses. They knew the challenges and obstacles before them but did not give up. I believe they were women of prayers so they prayed and decided to come before Moses in the presences of the priest, princes and all the dignitaries of the Hebrews. Moses had no way to reject but to receive them. Moses said I would bring your request before God. Moses was so wise for he did not want any man to stand against him on this matter. God said listen to the children for they are right. These Ladies were brave enough to change their destinies. What they did was enacted in the status of Israel. God told Moses to let their act become a statues or a decree, or law, so that if a man die and has no son then his inheritance should be passed on to the daughters, the nearest in kin comes in when there are no children at all. The daughters of Zelophad are the champion of women's right, in the time of Moses, even before the enactment of 1975 women's right. Satan will do his best to destroy your destiny but if you humbly come before the Living God, He is able to set things right, so that you will be able to achieve your God given destiny.

David also was able to achieve his God given destiny in the face of numerous oppositions. First, when he was just a teenager, he was able to change the destiny of the whole nation Israel by killing Goliath. During the reign of King Saul, the Philistines were a thorn in the flesh of the Israelites. They were always fighting with the Israelites. In one such battle, the champion of the Philistines, name Goliath, would come out of their hide outs and cursed the Israelites for over forty days and there was no one to challenge him. This story can be found in 1 Samuel 17: 1-2 "Now the Philistines gather together their armies to battle, and were gathered together at Shochoh, which belong to Judah, and pitched between Shochoh and Azekah, in Ephesdammin. And Saul and the men of Israel were gathered together and pitched by the valley of Elah, and set the battle in array against the Philistines. (In verses 1 to 2, the Israelites had already accepted defeat. The battle was being fought in the land of Judah, which belong to the Israelites. The Philistines were very strong and knew they would be able to defeat the Israelites. This is how Satan operates, he will always come to your turf if you allow him. The Children of God should not allow the enemy to encroach on our door steps, rather we should give the enemy no room to breath. We should attack the enemy in his territory. We can do this by praying without ceasing. The Philistines had decided the battle field so they could decide how they were going to fight the battle.) 1Samuel 17:3-4 "And the Philistines stood on a mountain on one side, and the Israel stood on a mountain on the other side: and there was a valley between them. And there went out a champion out of the camp of the Philistines, named Goliath, of Gath, whose height was six cubits and a span. (King Saul and his armies had accepted defeat, for fighting the battle in Judah, secondly, they saw Goliath as a champion and forgot about the God of Israel. They were not walking by faith in the God of Israel but they were walking by what they saw. This is the problem. For many Christians are moved by circumstances and not by faith in the Word of God. They saw the enemy as the champion, therefore they were already defeated. The point is your situation will not change if you see the enemy as a champion. Let say, someone may have a high blood pressure and instead of taking good medication and trusting God for the pressure to come down, such a person started calling this disease, my high blood pressure. If you start to personify a disease, like my cancer, my asthma, then it means, you like the disease. It is not yours, note Jesus Christ has already paid for our sickness, for by the stripes he received before he went to the cross. Do not allow the enemy to tell you that your sickness can never be healed. Our God is the same yesterday, today and forever, He healed yesterday, and He is in the healing business today and forever.) 1Samuel 17:5-7 "And he had an helmet of brass upon his head, and he was armed with a coat of mail; and the weight of the coat was five thousand shekels of brass. And he had greaves of brass upon his legs, and a target of brass between his shoulders. And the staff of his spear was like waver's beam; and his spear's head weighed six hundred shekels of iron: and one bearing a shield went before him." (Goliath was tall and well built. He had prepared himself for war, well dressed, with his face being the only part of the body that was exposed. No one in the armies of Israel could challenge him to a fight. A look at Goliath scared every Israelites, and they forgot the God who delivered their fore fathers from Egypt, the house of bondage. If you look at the circumstance, then you will always be defeated. When Peter was walking on the sea, as long as he fixed his eyes on Jesus then he could walk but as soon as Peter looked at his surroundings, he started to sink. Peter had to cry out to Jesus to save him. As Christians, we need to fix our eyes on the Lord Jesus.) 1 Samuel 17:8-11 "And he stood and cried unto the armies of Israel, and said unto them, why are ye come out to set your battle in array? Am I not a Philistine and ye are the servants to Saul? Choose ye a man for you, and let him come down to me. If he be able to fight with me, and to kill me, then will we be your servants; but if I prevail against him, and kill him, then shall ye be our servants, and serve us. And the Philistine said, I defy the armies of Israel this day; give me a man, that we may fight together. When Saul and all Israel heard those words of the Philistine, they were dismayed, and greatly afraid. (Goliath was arrogant and proud, as he challenged the Israel army to send a man to fight him. He knew no one would come against him as they were all afraid. Goliath saw the Israelites as servants of Saul and not the children of God. Do not see yourself as Satan see you but see yourself as God sees you. Goliath saw them as armies of Israel and not as armies of the Living God. The enemy will always try his best to belittle you and give you low-self esteem. The enemy will let you feel that you are good for nothing and you will not be able to accomplish anything in this world. Do not give in to the lies of the enemy, for you are precious in the eyes of God, and you will be able to do all things through Christ who strengthens you. For forty good days, no one was able to challenge Goliath, for the Israelites were greatly afraid, for what they heard Goliath said. Faith comes by hearing and hearing by the Word of God. The word of Goliath gave the Israelites a negative faith and they were afraid of Goliath. We need to build up our faith in the Word of God, and not what others are saying. Some people may say that you are good for nothing, but the Word of God says you can do all things through Christ who strengthens you.) 1Samuel 17: 12-15 "Now David was the son of that Ephrathite of Bethlehem-judah, whose name was Jesse; and he has eight sons: and the man went among men for an old man in the days of Saul. And the three eldest sons of Jesse went and followed Saul to battle: and the name of his three sons that went to the battle were Eliab the first born, and next unto him Abinadab, and the third Shammah. And David was the youngest: and the three eldest followed Saul. But David went and returned from Saul to feed his father's sheep at Bethlehem. (The first three sons of Jesse, knew the God of Israel but have no personal relationship with the God of their father. These three sons of Jesse had no personal experience with the God of Israel. If you have personal encounter with the Lord, you are different from the person who know the Lord but has no personal encounter with the Lord. The three sons of Jesse like the rest of the Israel army saw the problem and how big it was, that they forgot about the God of Israel. They saw things with their sight and their spiritual eyes were blind. They were well build, strong and tall to be in the Israel army but they were dumb and good for nothing. David was too small to join the army but he had what it takes to kill Goliath. David had a personal relationship and experience with the God of Israel. He knew the might and power of his God.) 1 Samuel 17:16-19 "And the Philistine draw near morning and evening, and presented himself forty days. And Jesse said unto David his son, take now for thy brethren an ephah of this parched corn, and these then loaves, and run to the camp to thy brethren; And carry these ten cheeses unto the captain of their thousands, and look how thy brethren fare, and take their pledge. Now Saul, and they, and all the men of Israel, were in the valley of Elah, fighting with the Philistines. (The Israelites were not there to fight, but to wait to be taken captives by Goliath and the Philistines. King Saul and his men were afraid and had no plan to fight the battle. In the face of war and trouble, they had forgotten to call their God. For forty days, Goliath had been defying and cursing King Saul and his men and Goliath just went away scot free. Let say if Goliath had taken Saul and his men captive, just after one week for not getting anyone to challenge him, what would have happened? No matter what, God had a plan for his people. God was going to send the teenager who will be able to trust on Him to kill Goliath, to set His people free, so that they could enjoy their God giving destiny. Jesse, the father of David wanted to know how his three kids were doing in the battle field so he sent David to send food his brothers and asked how they were faring, but God had a different task for David. David was to change the destiny of King Saul and the whole nation of Israel. 1Samuel 17:22-24 "And David left his carriage in hand of the keeper of the carriage, and ran into the army, and came and saluted his brethren. And as he talked with them, behold, there came up the champion, the Philistine of Gath, Goliath by name, out of the armies of the Philistines, and spake according to the same words: and David heard them. And all the men of Israel, when they saw the man, fled from him, and were sore afraid." (David came to the battle field and started talking to his brothers. At the same time, Goliath came out as he had done before to defy the Israeli army. David heard the same words from Goliath but was not afraid of him why? David had an encounter with the God of Israel. David had seen the mighty hand of God fighting his battles for him. David knew God had done it before and He would do it again. The men of Israel ran away from Goliath and they were very much afraid. David was not afraid and he knew he could get rid of Goliath.) 1Samuel 17:26 "And David spake to the men that stood by him, saying, what shall be done to the man that killeth this Philistine, and taketh away the reproach from Israel? For who is this uncircumcised Philistine, that he should defy the armies of the living God." (The men of Israel saw themselves as Goliath called them. They were the servants of Saul, and the armies of Israel. They saw Goliath as a champion, that was why they were afraid. David saw Goliath as uncircumcised Philistine. Which means Goliath was nobody who had no covenant with the Living God. Circumcision was a covenant God made between Abraham and his family, which were the children of Israel. David is saying, I have a covenant with the Living God, but this Philistine does not. Goliath saw them as servants of Saul and Israeli army but David saw them as the Army of the Living God. How you see yourself in the Lord Jesus is very important. We are sitting with Christ Jesus in high places where principalities and power are under our feet. Why should we be afraid of what the devil and his forces are doing. We are victorious and we need to walk daily in victory. We need to know the word of God and applied the word in every situation in which we find ourselves. I was once sick and my blood pressure was 220/117 and an ambulance sent me to the emergency. My children were crying for they thought I was going to die. I said "I would not die but live and declare the works of the Lord Psalm 118:17. I am still living and giving glory to God. If we know who we are in the Lord, we will be able to do things that are impossible. For forty days no one was able to go forward and fight Goliath, then, David came to the scene, and he was prepared to face Goliath. What was impossible for King Saul and his men was possible with David, why? David had a personal relationship with the God of Israel. David knew how to trust on God to fight the battles of life. It is easy to forget about God when you are faced with numerous problems and you may start to find you own ways and methods to solve the problems. David elder brothers saw David as an arrogant who had nothing to do but to watch the battle. Looking at 1 Samuel 17:28-29 "And Eliab his eldest brother heard when he spake unto the men; and Eliab anger was kindle against David, and he said, why camest thou down hither? And with whom hast thou left those few sheep in the wilderness? I know thy pride and the naughtiness of thine heart; for thou are come down that thou mightiest see the battle. And David said, what have I now done? Is there not a cause?" David brothers saw him as a good for nothing, arrogant boy who had left the sheep under no one's care and had come to the battle field on his own accord. I liked how David answered his elder brother; "is there not a cause?" Yes there was a reason why David's father sent him to the battle field. David was to go there and gave some food to his brothers but God had other plans. Whatever situation you find yourself, God has a reason, and until you find it, you will not be able to see the plan of God for your life. David knew he was there to fight Goliath and deliver King Saul and the nation of Israel from the hands of the Philistines. David was able to kill a lion and a bear, which came after the sheep, which, David was taking care. David trusted on the Lord to do that so he knew the God who helped him to kill the lion and bear would also help him to kill the uncircumcised Philistine. David was able to kill Goliath to change the destiny of the whole nation, and this act was a step toward his God given destiny of becoming the king of Israel. We need to trust on God for what He has destine for our lives to come to pass or the devil will make it impossible for our destiny to come to pass. Looking at Jeremiah 29:11 "For I know the thoughts that I think towards you, saith the Lord, thoughts of peace and not of evil, to give you an expected end." God has a plan for our lives and He is prepared to help us achieve our heights but we need to surrender our will to Him.

LIVING A VICTORIOUS LIFE IN CHRIST JESUS

Satan and his forces are doing their best to fulfill their diabolic mission on earth. John 10:10 "The thief cometh not, but to steal, and to kill, and to destroyed; I am come that they might have life, and that they might have it more abundantly." Satan is using any means fair or foul to get his wishes fulfilled. His aim is to steal, stealing your joy, health, money, and anything he can lay his hand on. He will also do his best to kill if he gets the opportunity and lastly Satan will destroy anything for example your marriage, your children or anything, which is very important to you. Satan is working with his demonic spirit to accomplish their work in this end time. Some of the spirit Satan is working with are the spirit of divorce, spirit of hate, spirit of miscommunication, spirit of violence, spirit of abuse:-(Physical, Moral & Spiritual), spirit of intolerance, spirit of poverty, spirit of homeless, spirit of joblessness, spirit of hindrance/ obstacle, spirit of recession, spirit of unemployment, spirit of hopelessness, spirit of frustration, spirit of depression, spirit of deceit \deception, spirit of hardness of heart, spirit of accusation, spirit of sickness/disease, spirit of low self-esteem, domineering spirit, spirit of anger, spirit of loneliness, spirit of destruction, spirit of death, spirit of wickedness, spirit of lying, spirit of cheating, spirit of sexual immoralities, spirit of homosexuality, spirit of pride/arrogance, spirit of pain, spirit of broken heart, spirit of disobedience, ancestral spirits, spirit of anxiety, spiritual blindness, spirit of depravation, spirit of defeat, spirit of laziness, spirit of jealousy, spirit of debt, spirit of defeat, spirit of disrespect, spirit of disappointment, spirit of schism/

division, spirit of devastation, spirit of confusion, spirit of fear, spirit of intimidation, spirit of lust (1 Cor. 10:6), spirit of seduction (1 Jn 2:26), spirit of discouragement, and unforgiving spirit. Satan and his forces are fighting a defeated battle, but they are not prepared to give up. We have already overcome the enemy through our Lord and Savoir Jesus Christ. Rev 12:11 "And they overcome him (Satan) by the blood of the Lamb, and by the word of their testimony;…" The blood that was shed on Calvary, speaks better things on our behaves and the blood has given us the victory over Satan and his forces. God, the Abba Father, has given us the victory through our Lord Jesus Christ, so as Christians, we need to walk in victory, no matter what Satan and his force may bring in our life. Looking at 1 Corinthians 15:57 "But thanks be to God, which giveth us the victory through our Lord Jesus Christ. The victory has already been won and declared so it is up to us to believe and march in victory in this life.

Endnotes

1 Edward M. Bounds, SATAN: His Personality, Power and Overthrow (New York, NY: Fleming H. Revell Company) Page14

2 Satan (New York, NY: Sheed& Ward) Page 11

3 Hans Kung, The church (New York, NY: Sheed and Ward) Page79

4 Satan (New York, NY: Sheed& Ward) Page31

5 Jeffrey Burton Russell, SATAN The Early Christian Tradition (Ithaca, NY: Cornell University Press) Page 16

6 Jeffrey Burton Russell, SATAN The Early Christian Tradition(Ithaca, NY: Cornell University Press) Page 97

7 Rev. Robert Antwi, Effective Prayers (Bloomington, IN: Xlibris Corporation) Page 94

8 Edward M. Bounds, Satan: His Personality, Power, and Overthrow (New York, NY: Fleming H. Revell Company) Page34

9 Awidi, S.K., Don't kill your Judas keep him (Accra, Ghana: Asatros) Page78

10 Satan (New York, NY: Sheed&Ward) Page 3

11 Rick Warren, The Purpose Driven Life (Grand Rapids, Michigan: Zondervan) Page236.

12 Edward M. Bounds, Satan: His Personality, Power, and Overthrow (New York, NY: Fleming H. Revell Company) Page 68

13 Edward M. Bounds, Satan: His Personality, Power, and Overthrow (New York, NY: Fleming H. Revell Company) Page69

14 Edward M. Bounds, Satan: His Personality, Power, and Overthrow (New York, NY: Fleming H. Revell Company) Page 76

15 William H. Hinson, Solid Living in a shattered World (Nashville, Tennessee: Abingdon) Page 52

16 Rick WARREN, The purpose Driven Life (Grand Rapids, Michigan: Zondervan) Page 175.

17 William H. Hinson, Solid Living in a shattered World (Nashville, Tennessee: Abingdon) Page 55

18 Edward M. Bounds, Satan: His Personality, Power, and Overthrow (New York, NY: Fleming H. Revell Company) Page38

[19]   Leon Cristiani, Evidence of Satan in the Modern World (New York, NY: The Macmillan Company) Page 156

[20]   Satan(New York, NY: sheed& Ward)Page 96

[21]   www.About.com

[22]   www.About.com

[23]   Author not known